SAS AND ELIT

Ropes
and Knots

Also Available from Lyons Press:

The SAS Combat Handbook
The SAS Fighting Techniques Handbook
The SAS Guide to Tracking
The SAS Mental Endurance Handbook
The SAS Self-Defense Handbook
The SAS Tracking and Navigation Handbook

SAS AND ELITE FORCES GUIDE

Ropes and Knots

ESSENTIAL ROPE SKILLS FROM THE WORLD'S ELITE UNITS

CHARLES STRONGE

Lyons Press

Guilford, Connecticut
An imprint of Globe Pequot Press

This Lyons Press edition first published in 2012

Published by
Amber Books Ltd
Bradley's Close
74–77 White Lion Street
London N1 9PF
United Kingdom
www.amberbooks.co.uk

Lyons Press is an imprint of Globe Pequot Press.

Library of Congress Cataloging-in-Publication Data is available on file.

ISBN: 978-0-7627-7803-4

Project Editor: Helen Vick
Designer: Graham Beehag
Illustrations: Peters & Zebransky
Picture Research: Terry Forshaw

All illustrations © Amber Books Ltd

Printed in Spain

10 9 8 7 6 5 4 3 2 1

DISCLAIMER
This book is for information purposes only. Readers should be aware of the legal position in
their country of residence before practicing any of the techniques described in this book.
Neither the author or the publisher can accept responsibility for any loss, injury, or damage
caused as a result of the use of the survival techniques described in this book, nor for any
prosecutions or proceedings brought or instigated against any person or body that may result
from using these techniques.

CONTENTS

INTRODUCTION

Although we tend to think of knots in purely practical terms, they have a significance stretching back into the mists of time. The ancient Egyptians were probably the first civilization to manufacture rope on an industrial scale; they needed large amounts of rope for hauling the huge stones that went into building the pyramids and other structures. The first recorded use of hemp, which was to become a staple for the sailing navies of Europe, was in China in about 2800 BC. The

skills developed by the Egyptians, Chinese and others gradually spread throughout the known world. Ropes and knots would have been used by the earliest fishermen for everything from making fishing nets and rigging to creating slings for glass pots.

Anyone who is involved in a range of outdoor activities will soon realize the importance of knots, whether they be for camping, climbing, sailing, fishing or outdoor survival. Our ancient ancestors would have used knots for building shelters or setting traps. For recreational purposes, their

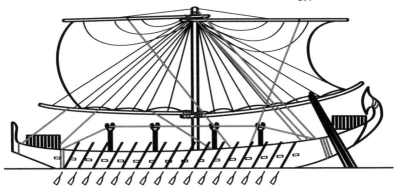

Egyptian boat

families would have applied knots in decorations, for braiding, platting and so on. Some cultures, such as the Chinese, even used knots as a way of recording information, and it is possible that China's early written symbols developed from such knots. There is evidence to suggest that the early Inca civilization also used a system of knots for encoding and presenting data – this 'language' of knot symbols was known as *khipu.*

Complexity of knots

Although it is often taken for granted that at a relatively early age we should be able to tie our shoe laces, the processes involved nonetheless require a particularly complex coordination between hands, eyes and brain. This most common of actions involves spatial awareness, manual dexterity, logic and memory,

and it remains a task beyond the most powerful robots. Knots have also challenged advanced mathematicians. The patterns in which they are tied and the reasons for their relative levels of efficiency are the subject of ongoing research.

The effects of knots upon the material in which they are tied, be it natural rope or man-made materials, is also the subject of investigation, for a knot almost invariably weakens the rope to which it is applied, no matter how efficient the knot. It remains to be seen whether science, including nano-technology, can produce a material in which the knot is no longer the weakest link, and may even be the strongest point.

Knots are like a language of their own, a script in rope, and they require practice to perfect, like good handwriting. Knots are rightly linked

Jury Rig

knots which they will rely upon while defying gravity, testing their physical strength and mental determination to the limit as they hang hundreds of feet above ground level on either sun-baked rock faces or ice-covered mountain sides. If a climber should fall, that same series of knot arrangements may save their lives, whether to the last anchor point in the rock face or to a belayer on the ground, all of which must have been tied on or knotted correctly.

When Thor Heyerdahl set about proving his theory that the South Sea Island had been populated by people from Peru, he created a seaworthy craft – the *Kon-Tiki* – that could have

to professionalism and expertise in certain disciplines. Sailors over the ages, whether in the merchant or fighting navies, would not have travelled very far without a good knowledge of knots. For sailors, knots could mean the difference between life and death, as lines and sheet needed to be secured correctly, lest a ship be left stranded in a confusion of flapping sails.

The climber's lifeline

Who more than a climber could claim to be at the mercy of the last knot they tied? For climbers, 'tying-in' uses the first in a long sequence of

been made by the inhabitants of modern Peru in about 500 AD. It was an important principle of the expedition that only natural materials would be used. Having travelled to the Peruvian jungle and cut down balsa trees to make the craft, he immediately secured the logs with tough jungle climbing plants before floating the logs down a river to a naval base. He applied the ropes and the knots, rudimentary as they were, that would have been used by people about two thousand years previously. Jungle lianas were also used by Heyerdahl to make the finished raft. Hemp ropes lashed together the nine logs that constituted the hull. There were no nails or any other form of metal or wire attachment. About 300 different lengths of rope were involved, each of which had to be securely knotted to bind the craft into a whole. The masts for the sail also had to be lashed together securely. Centre boards were bound into place, providing small keels for directional stability. It goes without saying that everything on this raft, including the lives of the men aboard, depended on the successful performance of the natural ropes and the knots that bound them.

Despite all the efforts of the voyage team, experienced seamen who came to see the raft before they departed said the ropes they had

Greek Trireme

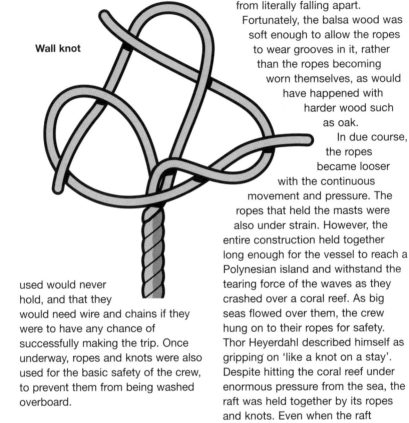

Wall knot

from literally falling apart. Fortunately, the balsa wood was soft enough to allow the ropes to wear grooves in it, rather than the ropes becoming worn themselves, as would have happened with harder wood such as oak.

In due course, the ropes became looser with the continuous movement and pressure. The ropes that held the masts were also under strain. However, the entire construction held together long enough for the vessel to reach a Polynesian island and withstand the tearing force of the waves as they crashed over a coral reef. As big seas flowed over them, the crew hung on to their ropes for safety. Thor Heyerdahl described himself as gripping on 'like a knot on a stay'. Despite hitting the coral reef under enormous pressure from the sea, the raft was held together by its ropes and knots. Even when the raft became a wreck, stuck on the reef, it remained intact.

I have described this adventure in detail because it underlies much of what this book is about—knots and ropes in practical contexts. The historical importance of knots is emphasized here as much as their importance in the present. The crew of the *Kon-Tiki* entrusted their lives to

used would never hold, and that they would need wire and chains if they were to have any chance of successfully making the trip. Once underway, ropes and knots were also used for the basic safety of the crew, to prevent them from being washed overboard.

Reaching safety

At sea, and having accustomed themselves to the movement of the raft and the difficulties of steering in rough seas, the team became fully aware that there was constant movement throughout the vessel, with some logs rising up, while others went down. The ropes held everything together and kept the raft

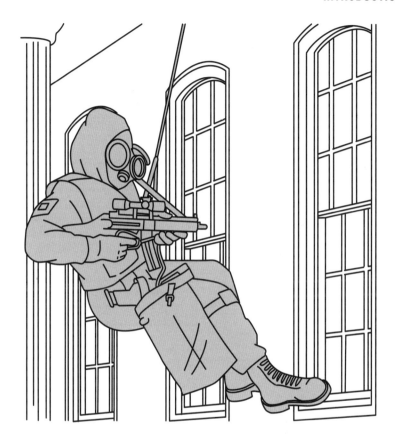

ropes and knots that would have been used in 500 AD.

Elite soldiers and special forces units across the world have also entrusted their lives to knots and ropes, as their specialist skills often involve mountaineering, advanced water craft and other relevant talents. The very same skills that were used in the *Kon-Tiki* expedition for lashing balsa wood logs together are also used by special forces and others for creating log rafts and shelters. Sophisticated deployment methods used by elite and special forces include fast-roping, which also involves an intimate knowledge of rope management.

There are many varieties of knot, and new knots and new ways of tying them are constantly being devised. There are books that claim to provide a comprehensive list of all the knots ever invented. This book is different, for although it provides an extensive directory of knots at the back, its main focus is on the sort of knots you would use in real life situations, and also in situations that involve risk-taking and survival.

The US Navy SEALs (Sea, Air Land) unit have to learn five essential knots as part of their basic training, these being the square knot (reef knot), bowline, clove hitch, right-angle knot and Becket bend. As the SEALs are one of the top elite units in the world, you would expect something a bit extra from their knot-tying skills, and you would be right. As part of their training, recruits are required to tie these knots in water at a minimum depth of 15m (50ft).

Going further back into history, when the Royal Navy dominated the seas of the world, one William Falconer, the son of an Edinburgh barber, served as a midshipman on Royal Navy ships in the eighteenth century, including as a midshipman on the *Royal George*. Falconer compiled *The Universal Marine* dictionary, which includes a number of the knots mentioned in this book.

Bowline

Good seamanship

If they were listed in Falconer's dictionary, it was because they were expected knowledge for anyone from an ordinary seaman upwards on one of the navy's ships. Here is the entry for the bowline, one of the most widely used of knots, which we will come across later:

'BOWLINE (bouline, Fr.) a rope fastened near the middle of the leech, or perpendicular edge of the square sails, by three or four subordinate parts, called bridles. It is only used when the wind is so unfavourable that the sails must all be braced sideways, or close-hauled to the wind: in this situation the bowlines are employed to keep the

Clove Hitch

weather, or windward, edges of the principal sails tight forward and steady, without which they would always be shivering, and rendered incapable of service.'

And you thought the bowline was just a knot …

Indeed, many knots have a long and distinguished history. We have already seen how the *Kon-Tiki* expedition would never have achieved or proved anything without knots. Many knots have a variety of names associated with their different historical applications, such as the manharness knot, artilleryman's loop, harness loop or manharness hitch— basically all the same knot, originally devised for dragging pieces of artillery. The knots could also be used for tethering horses.

Not all the historical terms have survived throught to the modern era. Although we are familiar with the general term 'hitch', some of the hitches used by navies of old are not so familiar, as the following quotation from an eighteenth-century British naval manual demonstrates: 'HITCHES. CLOVE-HITCH is two half hitches, one at the back of the other, made by the rattlings round the shrouds, and by buoy ropes round the anchors. BLACKWATER HITCH. Take the end of a rope, or fall of a tackle, round the back of a tackle hook, and jamb it underneath the standing part. HALF-HITCH. Pass the end of a rope over the standing part, and through the bight, and lay it up to the standing part; and repeat it for two half hitches. MAGNUS HITCH.

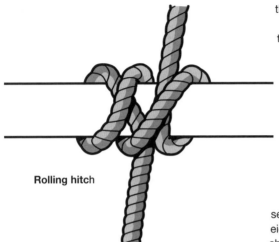

Rolling hitch

the end over the hauling part, and pass it through the bight; then take several turns round the standing part, and stop the end. The bigth serves as a sling for bales, drawing of timber &c.'

This is just one entry in the book, which provides comprehensive coverage of rigging and seamanship for the British eighteenth-century navy. It shows us again that the correct use of knots, each knot adapted for different purposes, was absolutely central to the successful performance of a ship, whether going about its ordinary duties or engaged in battle. Like the US Navy SEALs, who learn to tie knots in difficult

Take two round turns through the ring of an anchor, &c. and bring the end over the standing part, then round the ring and through the bight. MIDSHIPMAN'S-HITCH. Take a half hitch round the standing part, and a round turn above the hitch, which jambs tight. It is mostly tied to make fast the sheets of sailing boats. RACKING HITCH, for shortening slings. Lay the bight over both parts, and turn it over several times; then hook the tackle through the bights. ROLLING HITCH. Take two round turns round a mast, &c. and make two half hitches on the standing part. TIMBER-HITCH. Lay

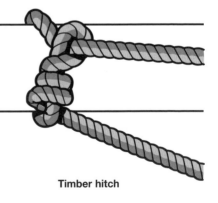

Timber hitch

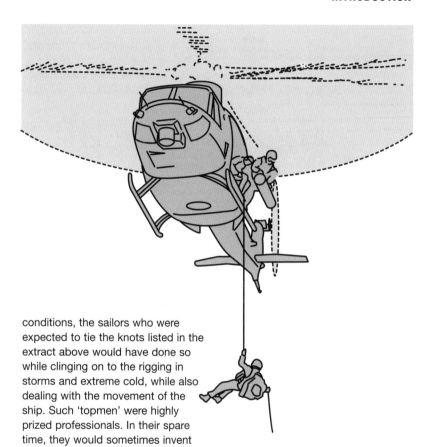

conditions, the sailors who were expected to tie the knots listed in the extract above would have done so while clinging on to the rigging in storms and extreme cold, while also dealing with the movement of the ship. Such 'topmen' were highly prized professionals. In their spare time, they would sometimes invent new knots for use in practical circumstances or pass the time making decorative knots.

Ropes and knots for survival

So, although knots seem in many respects to be basic to our human civilization and development, linking us to ancient history, they continue to be highly technical tools that must be

learned by military and naval personnel, climbers and sailors, in order to carry out complex tasks where risk to life is involved. Fumbling with knots or getting them wrong is simply not an option for professionals in a survival or emergency situation. This book will cover many of the most practical ways in which these knots are used in action.

Natural sources of rope

All sorts of natural fibres are used to create ropes with, and plants are one of the main source materials.

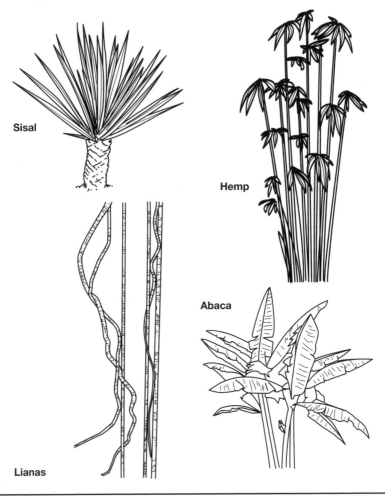

Sisal

Hemp

Abaca

Lianas

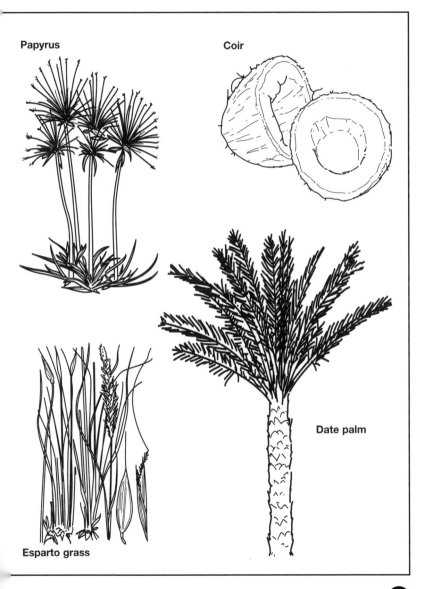

Papyrus

Coir

Date palm

Esparto grass

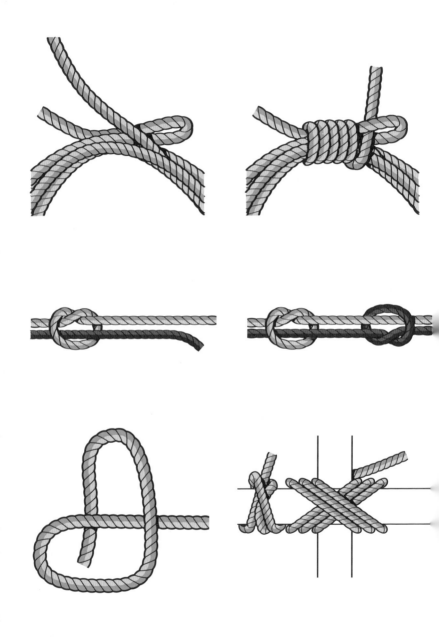

Rope has been made since ancient times from a range of natural materials. As mentioned in the introduction, natural lianas from the jungle and hemp rope proved to be adequate in holding a raft together for a major sea journey. Flax, papyrus, sisal, manila, coir (coconut hair), horse and camel hair, date palms, reeds, esparto grass, wool and silk are some of the variety of natural fibres available. Hemp rope is made from the leaves of sisal and abaca plants. Hemp was used by navies over the centuries and it was a vital part of national security that hemp should be procured so that ships could function properly. Due to the fact that natural rope fibres tend to wear relatively quickly and to be affected by exposure to water, those responsible for ship supplies were constantly on the look out for supplies from places as far afield as Italy and Russia. For the British Royal Navy, the best quality hemp came from the Baltic.

The invention of man-made fibre ropes and cords meant that a number of issues connected with

• •

A knot is a method of fastening or securing linear material such as rope by tying or interweaving. It may consist of a length of one or several segments of rope, string, webbing, twine or strap.

1

Knots are essential in many activities. Even simple tasks such as running a load from the hardware store to home can turn into disaster if a clumsy twist in a cord passes for a knot.

Basic Ropecraft

Types of rope

Common materials for rope include natural fibres such as manila hemp, hemp, linen, cotton, coir, jute, and sisal.

- **Nylon** is the strongest of all ropes in common use. When stretched it has a 'memory' for returning to its original length. It does not float so is ideal for maritime use, e.g. with anchors.
- **Polyester** is very close to nylon in strength when a steady force is applied. However, unlike nylon, polyester stretches very little and therefore cannot absorb shock loads as well.
- **Polypropylene** is the only rope which floats. For this reason, it is very popular for pool markers and water sports.
- **Manila** is a hard natural fibre especially resistant to sunlight. It is very popular for public utility construction and repair because it will not melt on contact with hot wires or equipment like synthetics do.

natural fibres were overcome. Man-made fibres were generally stronger, less prone to wear, absorbed water less and were less likely to be affected by mildew. From the invention of nylon in the 1930s, the range of man-made fibres has grown to include polyamide, polyester, polypropylene and polyethylene. One of the latest materials to be used in rope construction is Aramid, a heat-resistant synthetic fibre also used in the construction of body armour, which is used as the core material, covered by a sheath made from another material such as Polyester.

The use of advanced man-made fibres has meant that ropes have generally become thinner, without losing strength in proportion. However, thinner ropes are more liable to breaking in extreme circumstances, such as when a rope is run over a rough edge. On the whole, however, a well made modern rope is very unlikely to break.

Of the natural fibres, the polyamides include nylon, which has maximum strength when dry, losing some strength when wet. Because nylon does not float, it is often used for shipping or boat use and it has an element of elasticity. Nylon is therefore ideal for a tow rope where its elasticity absorbs some of the shock when the load is taken up.

Polyester, although it does not stretch as much as nylon rope, retains its strength when wet. Like

Overhand knot

This is a basic knot to learn and forms the basis of many other knots. It can be tied in thread as well as rope and is generally secure.

nylon, it does not float and it is generally hard-wearing.

Polypropylene rope varies according to the way it is constructed but in general it is used where it is useful for the rope to float, such as a line to a rescue buoy. They are also used as mooring lines.

Construction

Rope is usually laid or twisted, with three strands given a right-handed twist. A right-handed twist rope is also known as a 'Z' twist, while a left-handed twist is known as an 'S' twist. A rope is built up from the initial fibre stage, through twisting these into yarns, which are then in turn twisted into strands. The strands can in turn be twisted tin a pattern of either three (hawser-laid), four (shroud-laid) or five (cable-laid).

The modern man-made fibre ropes are made in a different way. Known as braided rope, this may involve typically an inner core of strands which are then sheathed with an outer abrasion-resistant cover. As with laid rope, there are variations in braided rope, namely single braid, double braid or solid braid.

Another form of rope is kermantle

Multiple overhand knot

This is one of many variations on the overhand knot. The multiple overhand knot involves several wraps, though it should be noted that it does not increase the diameter of the knot.

A

B

C

D

rope, whose particular construction lends itself to climbing and other activities, such as sailing, where a strong, reliable rope is required.

Kermantle ropes are often used for climbing and are often constructed in such a way as to create an element of stretch, in order to absorb shock loads. Kermantle ropes are also available without the stretch quality.

Going beyond normal usage, plaited ropes are usually sets of

Figure of eight knot

This knot is a mainstay in both the climbing and sailing worlds. It is mainly used as a stopper knot and has the advantage over the overhand knot of not jamming when placed under strain.

A

B

C

either eight or sixteen nylon ropes that are woven together in pairs to form equipment for mooring large ships and similar uses.

Tools

There are a variety of tools specific to rope making whereas some, such as pliers, scissors or needles, are more familiar. Gripfids and Swedish fids are used for prising apart rope strands or pulling strands through knots. A marline spike can be used for splicing wire and wire loops can be used in a similar way to fids.

Rope care

It is important to both store rope and coil it in the right way so as to avoid the dangers, particularly for natural fibres, of damp and also a whole range of other harmful effects, such as exposure to chemicals or extreme cold. Apart from anything else, a correctly coiled rope should be efficient to use when required, as for example when throwing a line from a boat. Ropes can suffer damage from being walked on or otherwise crushed in any way. The lifespan of a rope can be extended by regular cleaning for washing, followed by careful drying, especially if the rope has been exposed to salt water.

The correct coiling of ropes is taught in either formal or informal boat and ship handling or in climbing.

Terms used in the tying of knots

The active part of the rope or cord used in tying is referred to as the working end. The static part of the rope or cord is known as the standing part. When a rope is looped round so that two parts of the rope come together, this is called a bight.

The good habits and discipline acquired are not just for show but have a practical purpose, to ensure that they can be used efficiently when required. The correct coiling of ropes for different disciplines will be discussed under the relevant chapter headings later in the book.

1. Stopper knots

These knots have a variety of uses. They can be used to prevent the end of a rope from fraying; for decoration; to provide a handhold, for example in a safety line; to provide weight at the end of a line for throwing or to keep it hanging straight; and to stop a rope from passing through a hole, such as a block on a boat.

Examples of stopper knots include:

a. The overhand knot, which is often used both as a handhold and as a stopper.

b. The multiple overhand knot is often used as a form of decoration.

c. The figure-of-eight knot is a very common knot, which is often used as a stopper.

2. Bends

A bend is where two pieces of rope are joined together on a temporary basis. They are usually tied with two pieces of rope of equal diameter, though some can be adapted for rope of different diameters.

a. Sheet bend: this is perhaps the most commonly used knot for joining two pieces of rope.

b. Carrick bend: this is especially useful for joining together large ropes or cable.

c. Fisherman's knot: this is a commonly used knot for joining two lines together on a boat or elsewhere.

3. Binding knots

As their name suggests, these knots are used for binding pieces of material together and they are often found in the construction of shelters or rafts (as will be seen in a later chapter).

a. Square lashing: this is used, for example, where two pieces of wood cross at right angles.

b. Diagonal lashing: used to bind two pieces of wood in a cross brace.

Sheet bend

This knot goes back a long way and has its roots in sailing where one sheet was joined to another. The knot is adaptable and can work equally well with sheets or ropes of different diameters.

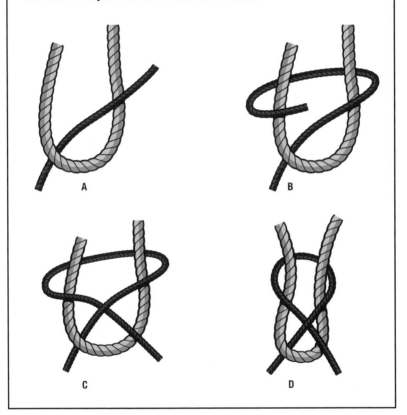

A

B

C

D

c. Sheer lashing: this can be used, for example, when binding the splayed wooded legs of a support.

4. Hitches

A hitch is a knot that is used to attach a rope to another object,

Carrick bend

This is an efficient knot for joining two lines. It has been found to be particularly useful when joining lines or ropes of a larger diameter and it will not jam even after being put under strain.

A

B

Fisherman's knot

This knot is an effective means of joining two lines of the same diameter but, due to the fact that it is effectively two overhand knots, it will jam when placed under strain.

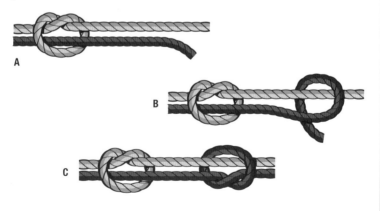

A

B

C

Square lashing

This is an essential knot for building structures with ropes and poles, such as rafts or shelters. The square lashing will bear loads effectively and keep cross members secure and steady.

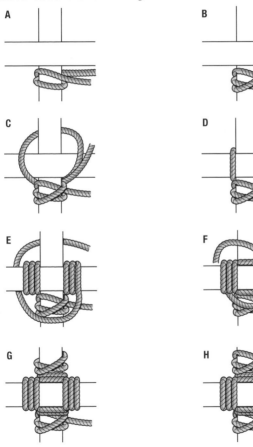

A

B

C

D

E

F

G

H

Diagonal lashing

This lashing should be used where poles are cross-braced at angles between 45 and 90. The diagonal lashing is started with a timber hitch to pull the poles together.

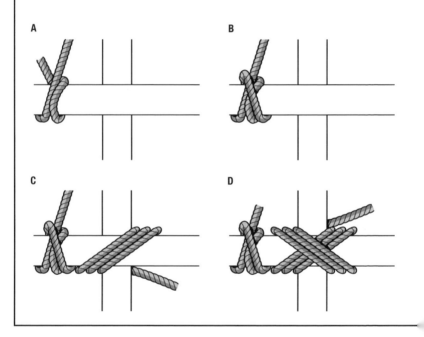

A

B

C

D

which can be a pole, a ring, a karabiner, a spar or a hook. Care should be taken to choose the right hitch for the job as some hitches are designed to be temporary while others are designed to be more secure. The security of a hitch can also depend on which part of the

rope or line the strain is on.

a. Rolling hitch: this is used to tie a rope to a pole.

b. Fisherman's bend: this is often used to tie a rope to an anchor or buoy.

c. Timber hitch: used to tie a rope round a log so that it can be dragged

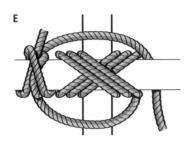

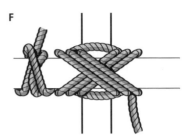

The diagonal lashing involves both wrapping and frapping turns. It begins with a timber hitch and is finished with a clove hitch.

without the rope slipping off.

5. Loops

Loops are a particularly useful form of knot that come in various forms and have various uses. A loop, for example, may be used to moor a boat; it can be tied round the waist

for activities such as climbing; it can be put through a ring; or it can be used for tightening, such as a noose or lasso.

a. Overhand loop: this is a straightforward way of creating a loop, though care should be taken to use the right kind of rope.

Sheer lashing

This lashing can be used either to increase the length of poles by joining two together or for structures which require the legs to be splayed, such as an A-frame.

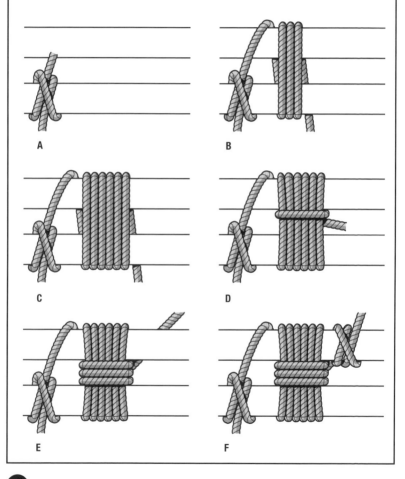

A

B

C

D

E

F

Rolling hitch

This knot can be used to attach a rope to another rope or to a hard object such as a pole. It is designed to provide a lengthways pull in one direction only.

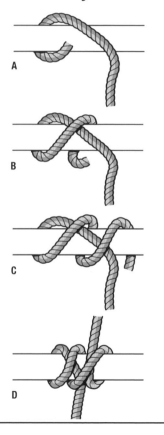

Fisherman's bend

This knot is also known as an anchor bend and is used for attaching anchors to warps. The knot is similar to a round turn and two half hitches.

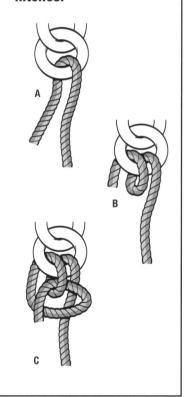

Timber hitch

This knot is useful to start lashings and it can also be used to drag or tow poles or logs. It is a relatively simple knot to tie.

A

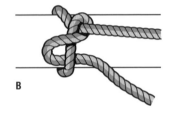

B

C

b. Figure-of-eight loop: this is a standard loop used by climbers to attach themselves to a karabiner.

c. Bowline: this is an ubiquitous knot used for such purposes as mooring ropes or forming a handhold.

As can be seen from the above, there is a type of knot to cover almost every need in a variety of outdoor environments on land or at sea. The practical importance of different kinds of knots was recognised by the founder of the Scout movement, Robert Baden-Powell, and they are regarded with equal respect by special forces and elite units today in specialist applications such as climbing or abseiling from buildings and helicopters. Knots and ropes will always be essential assets in outdoor and action environments.

Figure-of-eight loop

This knot can either be tied in the bight and then something passed through the loop or it can be tied around something such as a ring.

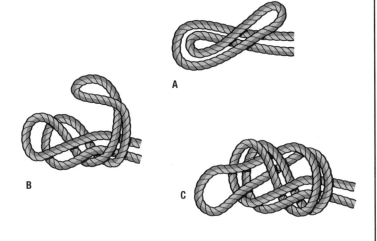

Bowline

This knot is used to make a secure loop at the end of a rope. It is a very useful knot that can be easily tied and untied and it is dependable when loaded.

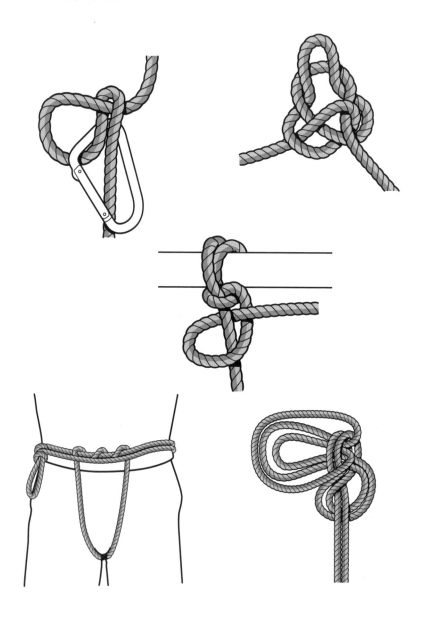

Elite troops and special forces around the world include mountaineering and advanced ropework as an essential part of their training.

In the Second World War, the newly formed US Rangers made their mark on D-Day by climbing the supposedly insurmountable cliffs of the Point du Hoc in Normandy and attacking the German gun emplacements there. Todays Rangers still carry out intensive mountain training at 5th Ranger Training Battalion (RTB) in Dahlonega, Georgia. The British Special Air Service (SAS) came out of relative obscurity and into the television limelight when they abseiled on ropes into the Iranian Embassy in London. Members of the Royal Marines Mountain and Arctic Warfare Cadre include advanced climbing as part of their essential training. Rappelling and abseiling are taught to legionnaires of the French *Groupe D'Intervention Gendarmerie Nationale* (GIGN). The US Marine Corps also include intensive mountain training on both an individual and team basis. The list goes on.

. . . .

Climbers use a number of essentials knots, and these can literally make the difference between life and death. Tying them correctly is therefore essential.

2

Climbers use a number of essential knots which can literally make the difference between life and death. Tying them correctly is therefore essential.

Using Ropes and Knots in Mountains

One of the priorities in training for climbing is choosing the right rope for the conditions and for the activity, whether it be urban abseiling, rappelling, rock climbing or ice ascents. The rope also has to cope with severe conditions and high-impact demands – most importantly, it has to have the capacity to handle the sudden shock of your weight if you fall. This event will create maximum shock loading both on the rope itself and on any anchors that may be involved, such as a belay anchor. Ropes should also be assessed with regard to their suitability for tying relevant knots and whether these knots will hold or can be untied easily.

A healthy rope is clean, pliable, resistant to water and with the flexibility to arrest a significant fall without causing undue harm to the climber.

There are two kinds of ropes for climbing – static ropes and dynamic ropes. The difference between a static rope and a dynamic rope is that one is designed for strength and stability while the other is designed to have a stretch that helps to reduce the impact on a climber should he fall.

The developments in rope construction over the years have greatly improved the safety of climbers, as old manila and hemp ropes were prone to snap under extreme fall conditions due to their lack of elasticity. Later, nylon ropes were introduced, which were an improvement, though these tended to produce side-effects, such as kinking when placed under shock loads. The modern climbing rope, known as kermantel, is formed from loose bundles of fibre surrounded by a braided sheath. Such ropes provide an adequate degree of stretch when shock loaded, without exhibiting side effects such as kinking or bulging.

Depending on the climb, it is important to decide on the correct length of rope. They can vary between 40 and 50m; longer ropes naturally have advantages in areas where an extra length of rope may come in useful.

Breaking Strength

The breaking strength of a rope is affected by a number of factors. Obviously, the rope needs to be well maintained. It should display any kinks or abrasions, or be subject to the influence of noxious liquids, extreme cold and so on. The critical factors in whether or not a rope will hold under extreme strength are the knots in it and also whether it is running over an edge. A knot will always weaken a rope to some extent, but a rough rock edge or a karabiner may also weaken it.

Ropes are designed with different potentials for absorbing energy from a fall. A rope with long stretch will reduce the impact of the fall but will

Iranian Embassy

In April 1980 the British SAS launched an operation to rescue hostages from the Iranian Embassy in London. Part of the attack involved abseiling on ropes from the roof of the building.

D-Day

US Rangers made a successful cliff assault at Pointe du Hoc during the D-Day landings in 1944. Rope ladders were used to scale the cliffs.

also allow the climber to fall further, to the point where they may hit a hard surface and suffer from injury. A rope with low stretch, conversely, may cause more discomfort for the climber by arresting them more abruptly, but will lessen the chance of the climber hitting a hard surface. The options need to be judged carefully, for a rope without enough 'give' could stop a falling climber so abruptly that it could cause serious internal injuries.

Fall factor

The fall factor is a way of measuring the severity of a fall and it can be calculated by dividing the length of a fall by the length of rope available. The fall factor measurement is normally calculated between 0 and 2 with 0 being acceptable and 2 being dangerous. Fall factors are influenced by intermediate protection, rope drag and other factors.

Static Ropes

The ropes used in climbing designed to minimize the effects of fall arrest are called dynamic ropes. Static ropes, by contrast, are also sometimes used in climbing expeditions but not in situations where they may be required to arrest a fall. They can be used instead for rappelling, mountain rescue or where pulling or lowering equipment is required. They are also sometimes used in carving.

Rope care

Due to their vital importance in climbing safety, ropes should be treated with special care in a mountainous environment. If a rope has been used successfully to arrest a fall, it may nevertheless be internally damaged by the extreme strain. Ropes that have been run for significant periods over sharp rock edges may also be damaged. Stepping on ropes can damage them, as pieces of grit are forced into the rope fibres, causing weaknesses. Stepping on a rope with crampons has an obvious potential for damage. Another potential problem is that ropes can be affected adversely by extreme cold, so care should be taken above the snow line.

Although a rope may well be re-usable when it has been applied in an extreme event such as a fall, certain checks should be made. The rope should be checked along its length for any signs of strain or damage. If there are knots in the rope, these should be untied with care, as the knots are likely to have been pulled excessively tight by the force of the fall arrest and the rope may have been weakened accordingly.

Ropes may twist and kink under use and it is advisable that any iregularities are straightened out before the rope is used again. Ropes can be used safely as long as sensible precautions are taken for as

GIGN

Special forces units such as the French *Groupe d'Intervention Gendarmerie Nationale* (GIGN) regularly practice techniques such as abseiling.

long as about two years, but this depends on the frequency of use. Five years of use on average is about the safe limit.

Rope Coils for Mountaineering

Rope management is an important aspect of mountaineering and an essential part of this is coiling the rope. A well-coiled rope can be carried easily, stored safely and be available for use in the most efficient way possible.

Mountaineer's coil

As its name suggests, this is a form of coil commonly used in climbing scenarios. To make a mountaineer's coil, grip the rope about 1m (3ft 3in) from the end and then use the other hand to produce a length of rope with both hands outstretched. Then bring a loop back into the other hand and continue the process until about 2m (6ft 7in) from the end of the rope. The first part of the rope is doubled back on itself and the rest of the rope wrapped round the coils. The rope is usually coiled in a clockwise direction.

Rucksack coil

First grasp the middle of the rope and then proceed to coil according to the method above. Once about 4m (13ft 2in) of rope are left, push a bight of rope through the coils and pull the ends through that.

Chain coil

This coil can be formed with either a single or a double rope. An overhand slip knot is tied at one end then a bight of rope is passed through the loop. The exercise is repeated until the end of the rope is reached.

Double hank/butterfly coil/lap coil

Start at the middle of the rope and put it one way and then another across the hand. Once the rope is almost fully coiled, the method of finishing is the same as with a rucksack coil.

Throwing a Rope

Before a rope is thrown, it is usually back-fed, which means letting it fall in a stack on the ground. This should be done in such a way as to minimize any kinks or twists. One end of the rope should then be anchored.

Holding the end of the rope that is not anchored, between six and eight coils are held in one hand and then placed on the ground. The process is repeated to create a second set of coils. The first stack of coils is lifted in the left hand and the other stack of coils in the right hand. The rope can be thrown either overhand or underhand, depending on the physical conditions. First the coils from one hand are thrown, followed by the coils in the other. Usually a warning cry is given to anyone who might be standing below.

Royal Marines

The British Royal Marines Mountain Leader Training Cadre are a specialist unit with expertise in cliff assaults and mountain work.

Tying-on

Tying-on to a rope can be done in a number of ways and will depend on whether or not the climber is wearing a harness and the extent and difficulty of the climb. In theory, the rope can simply be tied round the waist and finished with a figure-of-eight with a stopper or a bowline. The danger of using a rope tie-on is that it can cause damage to internal organs in a fall, as well as other complications.

Usually climbers will wear one of a variety of harnesses that provide greater comfort and protection in the event of a fall. Most harnesses used by climbers are seat harnesses, involving a waist strap and thigh loops. There is also the alternative full-body harness, which goes round the shoulders and chest and is tied on at a higher point. This configuration means that in a fall, especially if the climber is unconscious, the head and upper body will be prevented from falling rapidly backwards from the waist, as they might do in a waist harness.

Seat harness

The seat harness is the most common form of harness used by climbers, though care should be taken to avoid inversion of the body if the climber is unconscious in a fall.

Full body harness

The full body harness provides the safest and most secure support in a fall, as the upper body is also supported, preventing back injury.

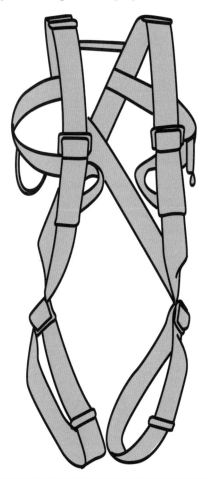

When tying on to a waist harness, the rope is passed through the waist and the leg loops, often using a figure-of-eight with stopper.

Although the harness may seem like a safe piece of equipment and that any potential problems may lie in the tying of the knot, in fact harnesses are susceptible to wear like anything else and can fail tragically if they are abraded.

There are a variety of ways in which the rope can be used to tie a belayer to anchors and this depends on the particular circumstances of the climb, the length of the rope and so on.

Single anchors

These include: a figure-of-eight on a bight tied in the rope and clipped into the anchor point; a clove hitch tied to the back bar of a karabiner.

Multiple anchors

Two anchors are often needed to provide sufficient security for a belayer. In order for this system to

Clove hitch

A clove hitch is an essential knot for climbers and is also important for other disciplines. The clove hitch can be tied in the bight and placed in a karabiner.

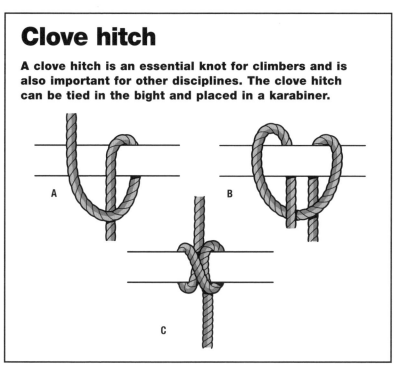

A

B

C

Figure-of-eight on a bight

This knot is often used to set up belays, or for rescue. The knot can be made in the middle of a rope and is an essential knot for climbers.

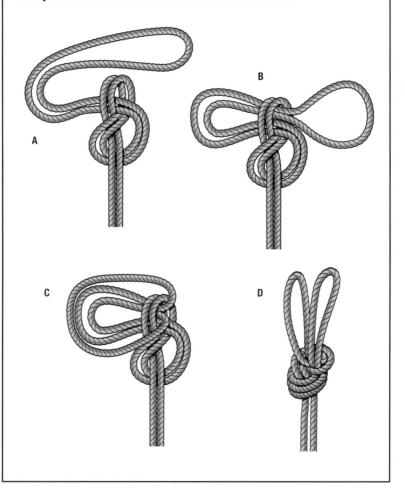

work efficiently, the load needs to be properly shared between both anchors, otherwise it will be the same as having two single anchors, both of which might fail consecutively.

Rope Systems

Climbers can use a variety of rope systems, depending on the complexity of the climb. The single rope system is the simplest, though the single rope system is not necessarily used on the simplest climbs. Paying the rope through the runners is fairly straightforward using a single-rope system, as is belaying. The limitations of a single rope system are revealed when the climb becomes more complex and when there is a risk of anchors being pulled out of the rock due to the angle of the climb and so on.

A double-rope system allows for greater protection, though it is also a more complex system which can cause problems if it is not planned and handled correctly. It is unlikely that both ropes will fail for the same reason, such as running over a sharp edge, which makes the double rope system safer.

Another option is to use two ropes as if they were one. This provides a backup against possible failure of a single rope.

Abseiling/Rappelling

This technique of descent is normally carried out with a double rope.

Abseiling is a useful technique for getting back down to the ground. When abseiling, a great deal depends on the secure fitting of the equipment and any attachments, and the quality of the rope. All parts of the abseil system need to work efficiently all of the time.

The climber needs to be securely attached to the rope and the rope needs to be securely attached to an anchor. The climber also needs to ensure that he does not run beyond the end of the rope. Natural anchors such as trees or rocky spikes can be used for abseiling. Failing that, the climber can use a number of pegs to spread the load.

The two ropes for an abseil can be joined using a double fisherman's knot. Alternatively, a double fisherman's knot can be tied on either side of a reef knot.

A hasty rappel is the simplest method of using a rappel rope. The system should be used as follows:

1. Roll down your sleeves and put on gloves.

2. Face slightly sideways.

3. Place the rappel rope across the back then grasp it with both hands, palms forward, with arms extended.

4. Use the hand nearest the anchor as the guide hand. Use the hand furthest from the anchor as the brake hand.

5. Lean out at a moderate angle to the slope.

6. Descend the hill facing

Royal Marines Commando Mountain Leader training cadre

In the Second World War a Commando Mountain Warfare Training Camp was formed at Braemar in Aberdeenshire in 1942. It was under the command of Squadron Leader Frank Smythe, Royal Air Force, who was a Himalayan mountaineer. The chief instructor was Major John Hunt, who would later lead the successful British attempt on Everest in 1953.

When the camp moved to Llanrwst in North Wales, its name was changed to Commando Mountain Warfare Training Camp, the new commander was Geoffrey Rees-Jones of No. 5 Commando. Here the Lovat scouts, a well-known regiment in the British Army, were trained in mountaineering skills. Another move south, this time to Cornwall, was made to prepare the Commandos for assaults on D-Day. Rees-Jones pioneered the concept of landing Commandos on rocky shores and climbing supposedly inaccessible cliffs. One of the cliff areas they trained on was the Carrack Gladden Cliffs at Hawk's Point in Cornwall. Small craft took the Commandos close into the cliffs and they attempted the climb from there. If the climbers fell, they would be lucky to fall into the sea, avoiding the rocks, and swim round to the nearest beach.

Geoffrey Rees later led a cliff assault on a German battery at Normandy during the D-Day landings.

The Mountain Leader Training Cadre is the Royal Marines development of the original unit which has a permanent staff of mountain and arctic warfare instructors. This unit is tasked with mountaineering duties, reconnaissance, rock climbing, ice climbing, route finding and extreme cold operations.

Later the unit became absorbed with the Brigade Patrol Group, which now provides reconnaissance duties for the Royal Marines.

sideways, taking small steps and maintaining an optimum angle to the cliff. Look downhill while leading with the brake hand.

7. Do not cross your feet and lead with the downhill foot at all times.

Braking a hasty rappel

1. To brake, the lower hand is brought across the chest.

2. The climber turns towards the anchor point at the same time.

Seat-shoulder rappel

1. Put on the rappel seat, roll down sleeves and put on gloves.

2. Place a steel locking karabiner on the rappel seat so that the gate opens down and away, otherwise the gate might open once the wraps are

Hasty rappel

A hasty rappel provides a means of descending a slope with nothing more than a securely anchored rope. The rappeler moves down sideways and uses one hand to brake, by pulling the lower end of the rope in front of the body.

Seat-shoulder rappel

The seat-shoulder rappel is considered a safer and more comfortable version of the body rappel. The rope is passed through a karabiner attached to a seat harness, then over one shoulder and along the opposite arm of the brake hand.

placed into the karabiner.

3. Approach rope with left shoulder facing the anchor.

5. Attach the rappel rope to the rappeller's hard-point karabiner: snap the rope into the karabiner.

6. Take slack from the standing/anchor end of the rope around the body of the karabiner and

back through the gate.

7. Ensure that the locking nut of the karabiner is fastened to lock the karabiner closed.

Braking

1. Lean back.

2. Face directly uphill while bringing the brake hand across the chest.

Seat-hip rappel

The seat-hip rappel system includes a snap-link inserted in a sling rope seat which is fastened to the person carrying out the rappel, providing optimum control.

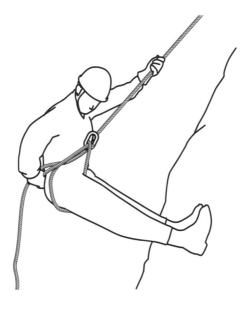

Seat-hip rappel

This technique involves the construction of a rappel seat.

1. Sleeves should be rolled down and gloves put on.

2. A steel locking karabiner is put on the rappel seat so that the gate opens up and away.

3. Step up to the rope with the left shoulder facing the anchor.

4. Snap the rope into the karabiner.

5. Take the slack from the standing end of the rope, make a wrap with the rope around the body of the karabiner and back through the gate. Check that the karabiner locking nut is secure.

Braking

1. Grasp the rope with the brake hand.

2. Place the brake hand in the small of the back, creating enough friction to stop movement.

A safety Prusik knot can be tied to improve the safety for the first person down on an abseil. The Prusik cord is attached to the hard point of the harness with a locking karabiner.

When abseiling, the legs should be at about 45 degrees to the rock and the body almost vertical. Walk backwards and control the speed of the rope by use of the brake hand. The feet should be flat against the rock and small steps taken downwards. Try to reduce the bounce on the rope by not jumping out from the rock, as jumping places a potentially dangerous shock load on the anchors, which may work loose and result in a fall.

Be aware that different types and diameters of rope, and different environmental/climatic conditions can affect the way the rope runs through the braking system.

Tying in the rope (end of rope)

1. Pass the end of the climbing rope up through the crotch strap, then through the doughnut and through the waist-belt tie-in point.

2. Tie the rope using a figure-of-eight, making sure the knot is as close to the body as possible.

Tying in the rope (middle of rope)

Take up a bight of rope and tie a figure-of-eight loop, then take a steel locking karabiner and attach the karabiner to the harness by securing the crotch strap, doughnut and the waist-belt tie-in loop. Then attach the figure eight loop to the karabiner.

Ascending the Rope

Ascending a rope can be a useful technique when a climber has fallen into a crevasse. There are a number of knots that are normally used for this procedure, though mechanical ascenders can also be used.

Dr Karl Prusik, an Austrian climber, invented the first ascending knot, which now bears his name, and ascending knots in general tend to be known as Prusik knots, even when they are variations on the original.

Generally, Prusik knots involve winding a thin rope round a thicker one, and the thin rope gripping onto the thick rope when force is applied. Specific cord can be taken for Prusik knots, but in an emergency boot laces or other slim cord can be used.

The sling of thinner rope should be formed into a strap. A lark's head is formed with the bight of the strap and two turns more are made with the bight. The greater the number of turns, the better the grip on the main rope. There should be no overriding turns and the cord should lie snugly against the rope. Ideally the Prusik

Klemheist knot

The Klemheist knot is a friction hitch that has the same purpose as the Prusik knot. The advantage of the Klemheist is that it can be used equally well with webbing.

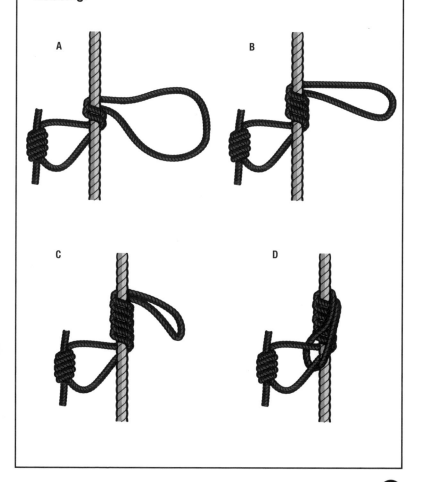

knot should be made using soft, clean cord. Problems may arise if there is ice on the rope and/or cord, as this may cause the knot to slip under strain. Ordinarily, however, the Prusik should slide easily up the rope when pressure is removed and should lock securely when pressure is applied.

Klemheist

This is a variation of the classic Prusik knot. A sling is passed behind the main rope, leaving a sling and a tail. Continue this process until only a small loop remains. The tail of the sling is then passed through the loop, and is pulled downwards to lock the knot in place.

Kreuzklem knot

The Kreuzklem knot is well known for its safety qualities and it is used by both climbers and by yachtsmen. It is similar to the Prusik and Klemheist knots.

A

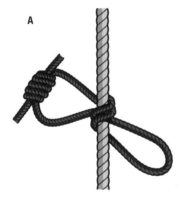

B

French Prusik

The French Prusik is a variation on the standard Prusik knot and it is also sometimes known as the AutoBloc. The advantage of the French Prusik is that it can still be moved when under strain.

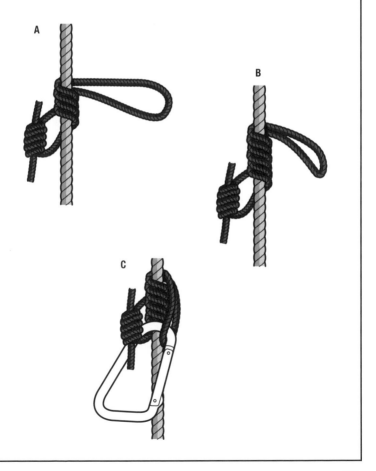

The Bachmann

The Bachmann knot is tied with a karabiner and is often used when the friction hitch needs to be re-set. The Bachman can be applied in incidents such as crevasse rescue.

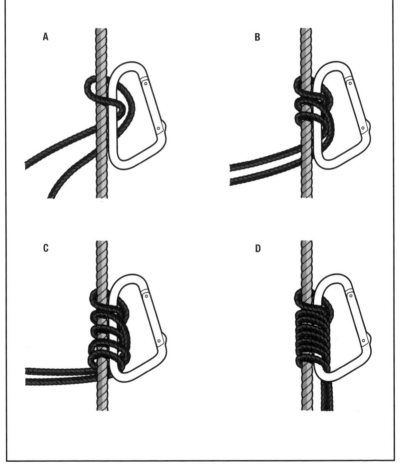

Kreuzklem knot

With this knot, the loop is wound up the rope and then down through itself. The advantage of this version is that it requires less cord to make, increasing the variety of cord that can be used.

French Prusik

This variety of Prusik is unique for allowing the knot to be moved while still under tension. It is formed from a short loop wound in a spiral round the rope, the two loop ends being then clipped into a karabiner. The French Prusik can be tied after three or more turns round the main rope.

Bachmann knot

The Bachmann knot involves the use of a screwgate karabiner. The karabiner is first clipped on to a sling which is then laid on top of the main rope. The long side of the karabiner should be held against the rope with one hand while the tail of the sling is wound loosely around the main rope and the long side of the karabiner. After several turns round the main rope and karabiner side, the tail is brought to the front. When tension is applied to the tail, the knot should lock, and vice versa.

Climbing Knots
The square knot

Holding one working end in each hand, place the working end in the right hand over the one in the left hand. Pull it under and back over the top of the rope in the left hand.

Place the working end in the left hand over the one in the right hand and pull it under and back over the top of the rope in the left hand.

Dress the knot down and secure it with an overhand knot on each side of the square knot.

There should be two interlocking bights and the standing parts should be on the same side and properly secured with overhand knots.

The figure-of-eight

This is a standard climbing knot that is used for a number of purposes, including tying on to the rope and attaching two anchors. It is often finished with a stopper knot.

To form a figure-of-eight, create a crossing turn and then bring the working end of the rope over the standing part. The working end is then taken behind the standing part and brought to the front of the knot. The working end is then passed through the crossing turn and pulled tight.

As the figure-of-eight is often used for tying-on, getting it right is essential because if the knot is tied incorrectly the climber could have a fatal fall. To some degree, there is a safety margin with this knot as it can turn into either an overhand loop or a figure-of-nine, if too few or too many turns are made. It remains

Square knot

The square knot or reef knot was originally used on board sailing ships to reef sails temporarily. This temporary nature means that it is not the most secure knot for tying two pieces of rope together.

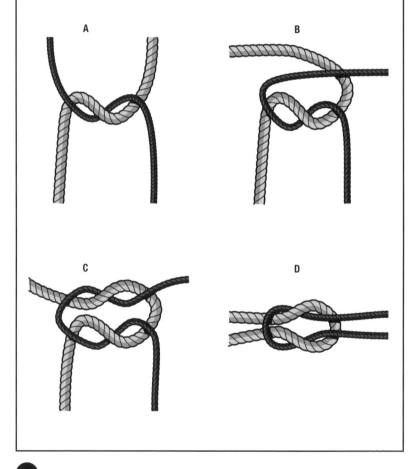

A

B

C

D

Figure-of-eight knot

The figure-of-eight is one of the few essential knots that both climbers and sailors should know. One of its most important uses is to act as a stopper. A key advantage of this knot is that it can be untied easily after being under strain.

A

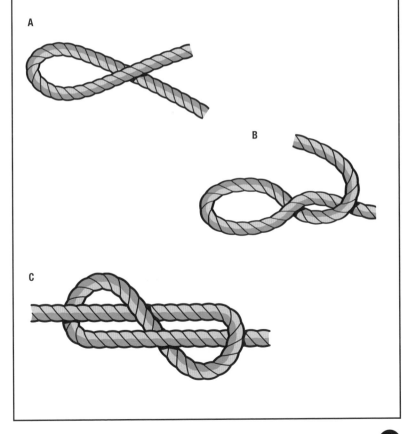

B

C

important to check the knot after it has been tied.

Figure-of-eight on a bight

This knot is used to form two fixed loops in the middle of a rope. The process of tying the knot involves a five-step procedure:

Using a doubled rope, form a 46cm (18in) bight in the left hand with the running end facing to the left. Grasp the bight with the right hand and make a 360-degree turn around the standing end in a counter-clockwise direction.

With the working end, form another bight and place that bight through the loop just formed in the left hand. Hold the bight with the left hand, and place the original bight (moving

Figure-of-eight loop

The figure-of-eight loop is a loop created out of a bight and can be used in climbing and other activities where the strain is moderate. When placed under strain the knot can be difficult to untie.

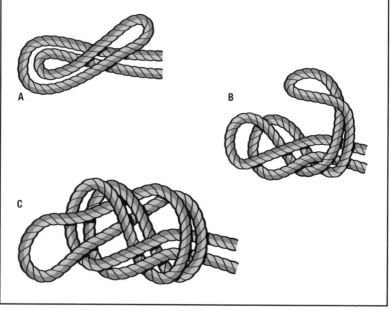

A

B

C

toward the left hand) over the knot.
Tighten up and secure the knot.

Figure-of-eight loop

This loop is a variation of the overhand loop and is easy to untie after it has held weight. The process of tying the knot involves a three-step procedure:

Form a bight in the rope about as large as the diameter of the desired loop. With the bight as the working end, form a loop in the rope (standing part). Wrap the working end around the standing part 360 degrees and feed the working end through the loop. Pull the knot together tightly. Make sure the ropes in the loop are parallel and not on top of each other.

Overhand knot

Also known as a thumb knot, the overhand knot can be either a stopper knot at the end of a rope after another knot has been tied or a handhold. Sometimes it is tied along life-lines to prevent hands slipping down the rope. The overhand is used in many other knots.

Double overhand knot

This knot is used as a more secure stopper. It is tied in a similar way to the standard overhand knot but the working end is taken twice round the rope before it is fed through the crossing turn. The knot should then be pulled tight.

Stopper knot

This is a variation of the double overhand knot and can be tied at the end of another knot, such as a bowline. Apart from acting as a stopper, it can also be used to add weight to the end of a rope that is to be thrown.

The knot is tied with a long working end. A round turn is then made round two fingers and the standing part and this is repeated for about five turns. The turns are then taken off the fingers and slipped on to a thumb, with the working end being pushed through the turns and then pulled tight.

Once the knot has been drawn tight, the turns can be arranged to ensure that they lie neatly alongside each other.

Round turn and two half hitches

This knot is used to tie the end of a rope to an anchor, and it must have constant tension. The process of tying the knot involves a four-step procedure:

Take the rope around the anchor from right to left and wrap down (it must have two wraps to the rear of the anchor, and one to the front). Run the loop around the object to provide 360-degree contact, distributing the load over the anchor.

Bring the working end of the rope left to right and over the standing part, forming a half hitch (first half hitch). Repeat Step 2 – the last half hitch

Overhand knot

The overhand knot is a straightforward knot that forms the basis of many other knots. It is difficult to untie when put under strain. It is sometimes used as the end of a rope to prevent it unravelling.

A

B

Stopper knot

This is a term used for any of those knots that prevent a rope unravelling or from passing through a hole. They include knots such as the overhand knot, figure-of-eight knot, stevedore knot and Ashley's stopper knot.

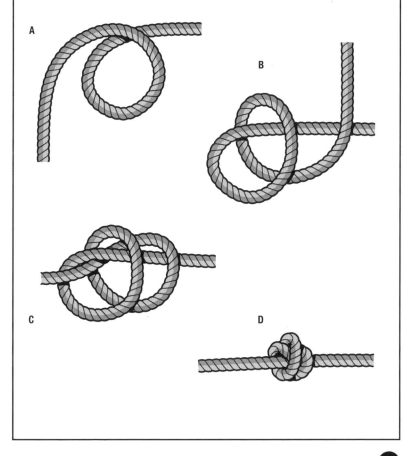

A

B

C

D

Round turn and two half hitches

This knot is used to tie a rope to an object such as a ring. A turn is made round the object and the two half hitches are used to secure it. Variations include two round turns and two half hitches.

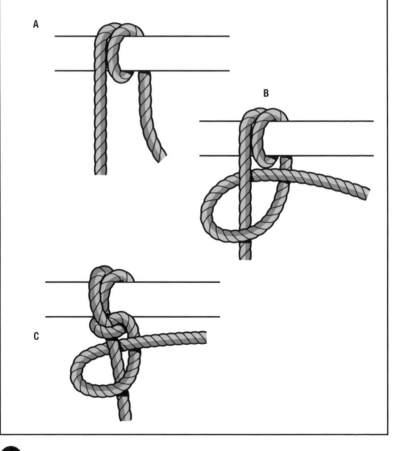

has a 15cm (6in) pigtail. Tighten up the knot so it is secure.

Bowline

The bowline has a high strength rating and it is also comparatively uncomplicated to tie. It can be adjusted easily and unties readily after it has been subjected to load.

Make a loop and then pass the working end over the standing part, turning the working end back towards the loop that has now been formed. Then pass the working end through the loop from behind. Pull the working end through the loop and turn it behind the standing part. Then bring the end round and back to the front of the loop before threading the end through the front of the loop. Tighten the knot, leaving a sizeable loop.

A triple bowline can be used with a rope to create a harness consisting of two loops for each thigh and one to go round the shoulder. The bowline should be finished with a stopper knot. This system can work quite well, as the knot will be above the centre of gravity, preventing the climber from falling over backwards.

Bowline on the bight

The bowline on the bight can be tied in the middle of the rope and it can be tied with either one or two loops.

Take a double length of rope to form a bight and then make a crossing turn by taking the bight over the standing parts. Then pass the bight through the back of the crossing turn. Pull the bight through and extend it just below the loop. Then pass the bight over and behind the loop and crossing turn. Bring it up behind the standing parts.

Fisherman's knot

This knot is also fairly easy to tie but it can work loose if not handled correctly. One way of preventing the knot from loosening is to tape the ends together.

The fisherman's knot is often used for joining two ropes together for abseiling, and for creating rope slings. It is best used for joining ropes of equal diameter.

Lay the working ends side by side from opposite directions. Take the working end of one line and tie an overhand knot on the other line. Make an overhand knot in the working end of the second rope. Pull the two overhand knots together.

Double fisherman's knot

The purpose of the doubling the fisherman's knot is to provide extra security, particularly when the ropes are slippery. With the double fisherman's knot, two turns are taken round the standing part when forming the two overhand knots. There is nothing stopping you from taking more than two turns for extra security. After the double fisherman's knot has been subjected to weight, it

Bowline

The bowline is one of the most essential knots and is particularly important for maritime use for making a loop at the end of a line. It can be easily tied as well as untied, and its only disadvantage is that it can come undone if not placed under strain.

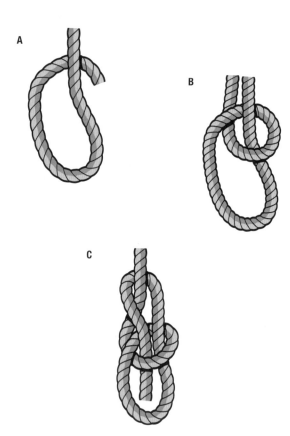

Bowline on the bight

A bowline on the bight is similar to the regular bowline, the difference being that the knot can be tied in the middle of the rope where it creates a pair of loops. It is relatively easy to untie after being placed under strain.

A

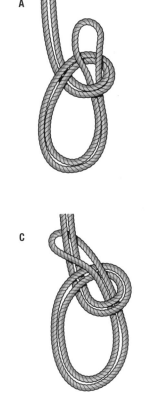

B

C

D

Fisherman's knot

This is another widely used knot which has a place in the top ten knots to learn. The fisherman's knot consists of two overhand knots tied in a symmetrical manner.

A

B

C

Double fisherman's knot

The double fisherman's knot is the version of the fisherman's knot that is most widely used in climbing and other operations where a very high degree of security is required. It incorporates a double overhand knot with each end tied round the standing part of the other rope.

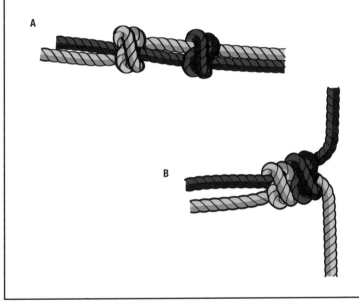

can be very difficult to untie, however.

Clove hitch

This is a useful knot but one that needs to be tied securely to avert the danger of its running when put under strain. It is not therefore a particularly secure knot. A clove hitch can be used in climbing, for example, to attach a rope to a karabiner.

Take the working end round the object to make a turn and cross the working end over the standing part. Carry on round the object for a half turn, maintaining the crossover.

Clove hitch

Another essential knot, the clove hitch is often used in a maritime context for tying fenders to a boat, lashing the tiller or attaching a rope to a post. It is used in other contexts as well, and is easy to undo.

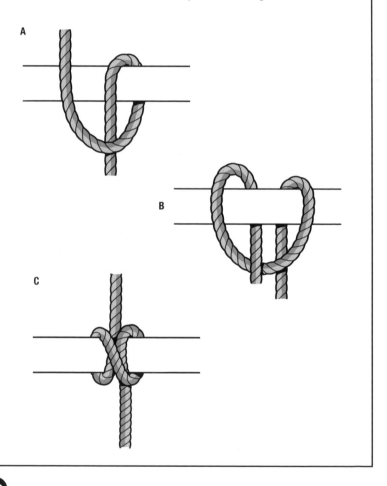

A

B

C

Bring the working end round and tuck it under the loop that has been made around the object. Work the knot so that it is secure by pulling on both the working end and the standing part.

Italian hitch/Munter hitch

This knot is used specifically by climbers to absorb energy when there is a fall. It is also used by climbers when abseiling. If the climber falls, the Munter hitch will lock in the karabiner.

To begin, make two turns with the rope, with the right strand on top of the left strand. Then fold the left crossing turn so that it lies on top of the right one. Open a screwgate karabiner and slide first the left then the right crossing turns onto the karabiner.

Once this has been done, the left rope can be the rope carrying the load while the right rope acts as the brake.

Tape knot/water knot

This knot, as its name indicates, is used primarily for joining tapes. It is also known as the water knot, for less obvious reasons, and as the double overhand bend. It can be used for joining ropes.

An overhand knot should be tied in one end and then take the working end of the second rope through and double the knot. Follow the route of the first rope to create double stands and then pull on the ropes on either

side of the knot to tighten it. You should leave long enough ends to avoid the danger of the knot unravelling.

Alpine/butterfly knot

This knot is formed in the middle of the rope and has the advantage of being untied easily after it has been subjected to load. It is also capable of taking the strain from either side.

First, make two and a half large turns out of a rope coil and the bottom of the outer left strand is brought across and into the centre of the two remaining strands. The left-hand passes beneath the other two turns. A bight is then pulled through, of whatever size is required. In order to tighten and secure the knot, both standing parts should be pulled in opposite directions.

Sheet bend

This knot is used for joining either ropes or tapes together. Ideally it should be tied with rope or tape of equal diameter. If this is not the case, a double sheet bend should be used for added security.

A bight is made in the end of one of the ropes and the second rope working end is pushed through the centre of the bight. The working end then passes under the bight and is tucked underneath itself. The two short ends of either rope should be on the same side. Hold the loop of the first piece of rope and the

Italian hitch/Munter hitch

This hitch is often used by climbers for belay systems. The purpose of the knot is as a friction device to control the rate of descent. The friction acts on both the karabiner and the rope.

A

B

C

D

Tape knot/water knot

This knot is often used by climbers to join two pieces of webbing together and it can be difficult to untie. The knot should be checked carefully and tails should be left long to avoid failure of the knot.

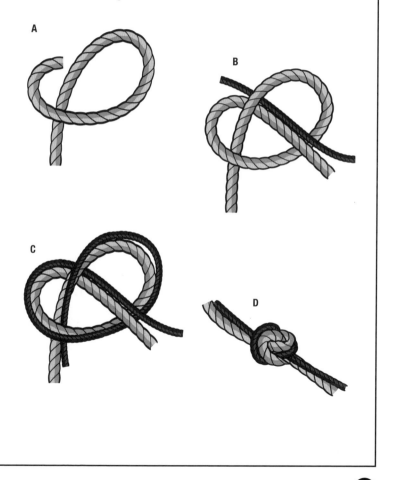

Alpine knot/butterfly knot

This knot forms a fixed loop in the middle of a rope and can be tied in the bight. It has a number of uses in a climbing context, including rigging and anchors.

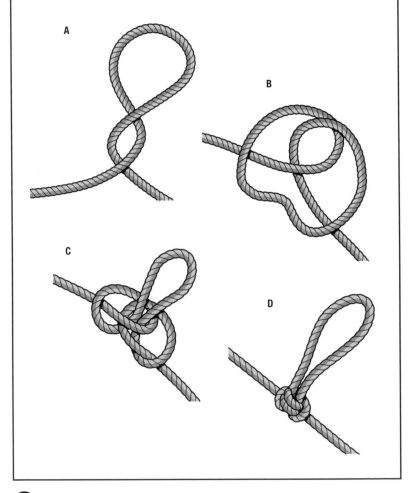

A

B

C

D

Sheet bend

This knot is often used in a maritime environment to join two ropes of similar diameter. It is more secure than a reef knot, but can come undone if not under strain.

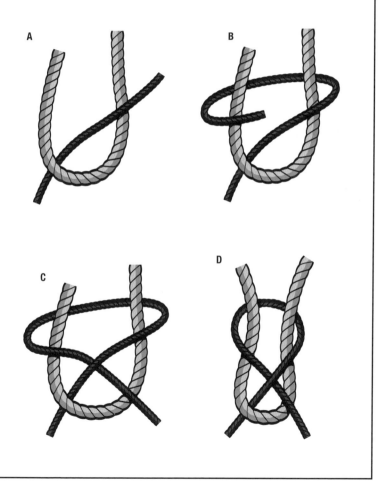

A

B

C

D

Lark's foot/cow hitch/ ring hitch

This is a simple knot designed to attach a rope to a post or ring or anything similar. The knot can either be tied with the working end or with a closed loop.

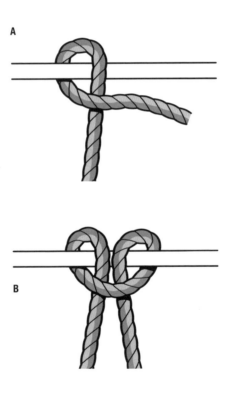

A

B

standing part of the second piece of rope and pull to tighten the knot.

The double sheet bend may be formed with two pieces of different diameter. The process is the same as described above in the initial stages, but the working end is brought around and under the bight and its own standing line again and then pushed through alongside the initial knot to make a double knot.

Lark's foot/cow hitch/ring hitch

This is a relatively simple knot, though for climbing purposes it is not considered particularly secure.

A bight is formed by doubling a piece of rope and this is then passed through a karabiner or other device. The standing parts are then pulled through the bight that has been formed.

Mariner's knot

This knot is sometimes used to relieve the weight of a fallen climber on the belay device. A sling with the mariner's knot can be attached to the anchors and it can be released even under strain. The knot is used almost exclusively by climbers, despite its deceptive name.

Make a bight in webbing and push it through and over the bar of the karabiner. Repeat the process to make a second turn round the bar of the karabiner. Pass the working end round the front of the standing part and then take it round the back of the standing

part. Repeat this for four turns. To finish the knot, tuck the working end between the two tapes of the standing part. The knot is held by the tension of the weight placed upon it, but it can also be easily released.

Wireman's knot

This knot creates a fixed loop in the middle of the rope. Facing the anchor that the knot system will be tied to, take up the slack from the anchor and wrap two turns round the left hand. When going round for the second turn, form a loop of about 30.5cm (12in) – this will create the fixed loop that is the basis of the knot. There will be separate turns in the hand. Take the middle turn and place it over the rear turn. Take the rear turn and place it over the front turn. Take the first turn and place it over the middle turn. Take the middle turn and pull it up to form a fixed loop. Tighten up the knot first by pulling on the fixed loop and the two working ends and then by pulling tight on the two working ends.

Frost knot

This is a simple knot designed to create a stirrup effect in webbing.

A short bight is made in one end of a length of tape or webbing and the other end of the tape or webbing is inserted between the two flat sections of the bight. Form a loop by going around anti-clockwise with all the parts of the tape or webbing held together. The parts are then taken behind the loop and then pulled through to create an overhand knot.

Specialist Techniques
Crossing the bridge

For this particularly useful traversing technique, the climber ties himself into a rappel seat and attaches a large steel locking karabiner with the gate facing down and away. Then the climber

Creating a rope bridge in mountainous terrain

A rope bridge can be used to cross an obstacle such as a ravine with a stream running through it.There should be secure anchors on both sides of the obstacle and they should be placed in accessible areas. A water obstacle such as a stream is first crossed by a swimmer, who takes with him the front end of a 45m (150ft) rope. Allow about a third of the available rope for tying to both anchors. The safety line team move up from the chosen site of the rope bridge and tie a figure-of-eight loop in the safety line. The swimmer puts his arm through the loop and swims across.

Meanwhile, the bridging team on the nearside wraps the rope several times round the anchor and finishes it with a square knot. Once the swimmer is across, the belay man on the nearside creates figure-of-eight knots in both the safety line and the main rope and attach the two with a karabiner. The swimmer on the far side then pulls the rope across, keeping the rope out of the water with the help of the belay man.The following procedure is then followed:

1. Once the swimmer has the end of the crossing rope, he attaches it to the far-side anchor using a tree wrap. Then the safety line is also secured on both sides. The safety line can be attached so that it is parallel to the crossing rope, especially if a fall from the main rope would be dangerous.

snaps the karabiner into the crossing rope. The climber hangs below the rope with his head towards the anchor on the far side.

The climber then pulls with his arms to move along the crossing rope. A pack may either be carried on the climber's back or it can be attached separately to the rope with a karabiner, the climber putting his legs through the straps of the pack to drag it along with him.

2. The bridging team on the nearside then take a karabiner and clip it to the nearside anchor. The bridging line is then clipped to the karabiner. A 1m (3ft) Prusik secures the bridging line to the karabiner with a French Prusik.

3. A French Prusik is then tied on the bridging rope as far away from the anchor as possible. A karabiner is then clipped into the loops of the French Prusik.

4. A bight is then taken from the running end of the rope and clipped into the karabiner hanging from the tails of the French Prusik.

5. Bring a bight back from the clipped-in rope to the anchor, take one karabiner and clip it into the karabiner on the anchor. Then take the bight of rope and clip it into this karabiner.

6. Take a 1m (3ft) Prusik and tie a French Prusik on to the bottom end of the bight clipped into the karabiner on the rope, positioned well away from the anchor. Take a karabiner and clip it into the tail of the French Prusik.

7. Take a bight of rope from the karabiner in step 6 and clip it into the karabiner from step 6.

Once this mechanical system has been constructed, a mule team or team of men can pull on the rope as strongly as possible to create maximum tension. The direction of the tension pull should be as far as possible in line with the line of the crossing rope.The team now has a rope bridge ready to use.

Mariner's knot

This knot is not, as its name suggests, designed either by or for sailors but it is used by climbers or rescuers. The knot can be released when under strain, so it can be used in self-rescue.

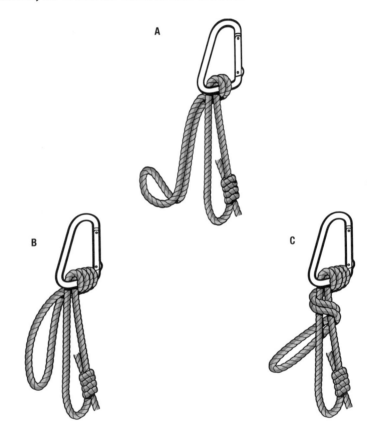

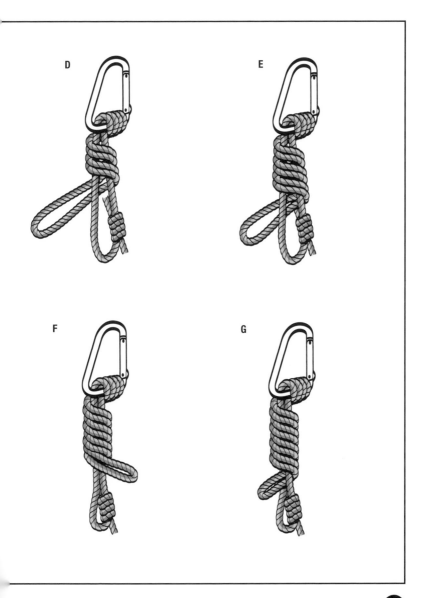

Cliff assault

Special forces, as mentioned before, are trained in the techniques of cliff assault. British Commandos developed cliff-assault methods when probing the coasts of German-

Wireman's knot

This knot is tied in the middle of a rope and forms a loop that can be used for a number of purposes, such as when constructing a rope bridge.

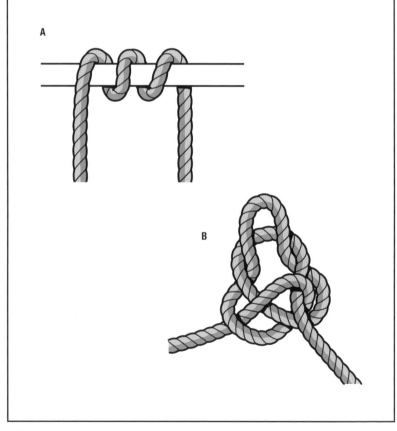

A

B

occupied Europe during the Second World War. Many of these techniques have now become standard.

In order for a cliff assault to be successful, static climbing ropes need to be installed and this can only be done by a team of highly experienced climbers who will not have the advantages of ropes themselves. The advance force will first establish bottom anchors and top anchors on the cliff face. There are a number of options after this action: the rest of the assault team can ascend by either a top-rope method, fixed-rope method or even via cable ladders.

Once the advance force has reached the top, they establish security and also communications with the team at the base of the cliff. They will also identify areas for rappel lanes, should a quick withdrawal be required. Whatever system has been agreed for climbing is then put in place for the main force at the base of the cliff. The system, whether static ropes or ladders, is tested for safety.

Once the main force has ascended, the advance force removes the ascending equipment and fully establishes the rappel lanes for descent. If the main force is fighting a retreat, a defensive perimeter is established and members of squads take it in turns to descend via the rappel system. At last, the advance climbers themselves will rappel down and retrieve the rappel lanes.

Fast-rope techniques

A now-familiar aspect of special operations and elite forces training is fast-roping as well as rappelling. The technique is used to deploy troops quickly onto the ground without having to land a helicopter. Fast-roping involves specialist techniques and also a number of knots that have distinctive functions.

Fast-roping is an easier and more efficient alternative to rappelling, which involves complex knots and anchor attachments. A wide range of things can go wrong with the rappelling procedure, especially under pressure in a hostile operational environment.

Fast-roping involves only one rope leading to the ground and the only bodily attachment points are the roper's own hands, knees and feet. The obvious down-side of fast-roping is that the roper is therefore more exposed to the danger of a fall, especially when carrying heavy equipment and when the helicopter may be moving erractically.

Since getting troops out of a helicopter and down to the ground is much quicker using the fast-rope technique, the overall safety of the crew and passengers is increased exponentially. There are a number of potential complications, however, that can arise when fast-roping from a

Frost knot

The frost knot is normally tied in webbing and can be used to bind an *étrier* – a set or stirrups that can be used by climbers to aid certain climbing techniques.

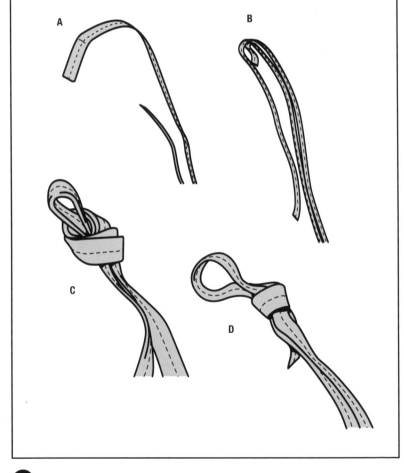

helicopter. For one, the pilot of the helicopter may need to manoeuvre suddenly to avoid enemy fire. As the helicopter moves away from the drop zone, the shift may also cause the rope to hang at an angle as opposed to vertically. The rope can therefore became tangled up with something on the ground. There is also a potential danger to personnel on board if they unhook their inflight safety harnesses too early, before the helicopter has finished manoeuvring (bearing in mind that the person descending needs to be unhooked first).

Other problems with fast-roping may arise at night when it is difficult to see the rope and the ground. In these circumstances, the US Marines use devices know as 'chem lights', which are attached at key points on the ropes so that the lie of the rope can be judged and also so the fast-roper can see where to grasp with his hands.

The knots used in fast-roping are divided into four main areas: end of rope knots, anchor knots, middle of rope knots and special knots.

End of rope knots
1. Square knot
2. Water knot
3. Double fisherman's knot

Anchor knots
1. Bowline
2. Clove hitch
3. Round turn with two half hitches

Middle of rope knots
1. Figure-of-eight loop

Special knots
1. Overhand knot
2. End of rope Prusik
3. Directional figure-of-eight loop
4. Military rappel seat
5. Round-body bowline with a figure-of-eight
6. Munter hitch
7. Three-loop bowline
8. Swami wrap

Three-loop bowline
This knot creates tree anchor loop points. Taking one end of the rope, fold about 3m (10ft) of line. Use the folded part and tie a bowline in the same way as you would tie a bowline with a single line. The bowline forms two loops while the running end forms the third loop. Then attach the three loops to attachment points using locking karabiners.

Marine/military rappel procedures
When a soldier intends to rappel over a cliff, building or similar feature, he is first hooked up, and with his brake on he goes to the edge and faces the anchor point. He then moves into an L-shaped position, with his legs almost horizontal with the ground and his back almost vertical.

Once the rappeller starts to descend, the belay man places the

Black Hawk Down: fast-roping in action

In October 1993, members of the 75th Ranger Regiment, Task Force Ranger, were deployed into Mogadishu in Somalia to arrest senior staff of the faction leader General Aideed. The Rangers were carried to the location in MH-60 Black Hawk helicopters and 7.6cm (3in) thick nylon ropes were let down to the ground. One of the ropes landed on a car and the helicopter had to manoeuvre to free it. Other small things went wrong: the strap broke on a Ranger's goggles and this incident made him forget to unhitch his ear phones when he stood up to head for the rope, ripping the ear phone cord out of the ceiling of the helicopter.

Then something very serious went wrong. Pumped up with pre-combat adrenalin, and perhaps put off balance by the movement of the helicopter as it adjusted position, one of the Rangers (Todd Blackburn) missed the rope and fell 21m (70ft) to the ground.

The rest of the team on the ground were coming under fire and they had to get the wounded Ranger to a medical centre urgently or he would die. He had serious injuries to his head and internal organs. Blackburn was eventually loaded on to a Humvee, which made a bid to return to base over land, but by now enemy gunmen were all around and the speeding vehicle became a target. The Ranger machine-gunner on the vehicle was shot in the head. Fortunately for the rest of the occupants, and for Blackburn, they managed to get back to base, where Blackburn could start on the long road to recovery.

This incident demonstrates the potential dangers of the fast-rope system in a real battle scenario and it also testifies to the commitment of the US Rangers never to leave one of their wounded comrades on the battlefield.

rappel rope high in his back, under his armpits, holding the standing end with his weak hand and the running end with his strong hand.

If for any reason the rappeller should lose control, the belayer places the running end of the rope on his chest and runs backwards to stop the rappeller from falling.

Fast-roping procedure
The fast-roping soldier accesses the rope from either a seated or a standing position, depending on the circumstances. If the roper is seated, the command to start is 'Feet, hands'. If the roper is standing the command is 'Hands'.

The roper is tapped on the back with the verbal command 'Go'. He turns between 45 and 90 degrees and descends the rope, maintaining control of speed through friction on feet, knees and hands (which must be gloved). If

From US Marine Corps

Helicopter Rope Suspension Techniques (HRST) Operations

Military rappel seat
The military rappel seat is made from a sling rope:
• Take the center of the sling rope and place it on the left hip so that the running ends of the rope wrap around the waist just below the hip bone.
• Bring both ends together in front of the body.
• Tie an overhand knot with two wraps in front.
• Bring the two running ends down through the legs, up over the buttocks, and over the original waist wrap and the waist.
• Bring the rope over itself forming a bight, then cinch the rope up tightly. Note: The rope should run along the outside of the buttocks.
• Take the two running ends and make a square knot with two overhands on the left hip.
Any loose rope from the square knot is tucked into a pocket. Pigtails will be a minimum of 4 inches.

there is too much of a burning sensation in the hands, more pressure is applied on the rope with feet and knees.

If the roper needs to stop on the descent for any reason, one foot is slid over the other, with the rope between them and pressure exerted on the rope. This can be accompanied by a wringing movement with the hands. Once the roper is about 1.5m (5ft)

from the ground, he spreads his legs slightly and bends the knees to absorb the impact of landing.

Special Patrol Insertion and Extraction (SPIE)

SPIE is designed for fast aerial insertion and extraction of special forces teams, such as covert reconnaissance patrols.

This system uses heavy-duty cargo

Iranian Embassy Siege: abseiling in action

On Wednesday 30 April 1980, the Iranian Embassy in London was attacked by six terrorists, and several of the staff and a British policeman were taken hostage. The terrorists threatened to kill the hostages if their demands were not met. Although the Metropolitan Police started negotiations, it became apparent that the situation was deteriorating. Unknown to the British public, the SAS had been put on alert and their commander flew to London by helicopter to recce the embassy building personally. Members of 6 Troop, B Squadron, 22 SAS moved from their base to a holding point in Beaconsfield.

Electronic surveillance was carried out on the building by the police and MI5, and the SAS themselves moved closer and carried out further reconnaissance and planning, utilizing mock-ups of the building at remote locations. A small team of SAS troopers also went up on to the roof of the building at night to conduct a closer reconnaissance.

By 5 May, negotiations were collapsing, culminating in the murder of one of the hostages. The police had done their best; now was the time for action. The Metropolitan Police

straps and anchor points to withstand the extra load pressure of an entire patrol hanging off the SPIE rope dangling from an aircraft.

The members of the patrol put on a SPIE harness, a process that involves passing the arms through shoulder loops and slipping the end of the chest strap through a chest adapter while ensuring that the strap is back-laced through the chest adapter for

quick release. The V-ring of each leg strap is attached to its respective ejector snap. Chest and leg straps are tightened for a good fit.

Safety line
During training for SPIE operations, a safety line can be added to the set-up, consisting of a rope under 4m (12ft) long and an additional karabiner. The rope is passed round

Commissioner formally handed control of the operation to the British Army, and the SAS.

The SAS assault plan included a simultaneous attack on both the front and rear of the building. At the front, SAS troopers were seen on live TV moving from the balcony of the building next door to an embassy balcony and placing frame charges against the windows.

At the back of the building 'Red Team' had set up two abseil ropes, which were then let down on to the balcony of the second floor. At the command, three four-man 'sticks' abseiled down the ropes. One of the soldiers accidentally smashed a window pane with his boot, making a noise that alerted the terrorists. The commander, however, kept up the momentum by ordering the full assault to continue.

Another member of Red Team became caught in the abseil rope and was suspended above a window. Curtains had caught fire from the stun grenades used in the initial assault, so he was in some danger of being burnt until fellow soldiers cut him down.

The rest of the assault went to plan, as the SAS troopers stormed through the building and cleared each room. Five of the terrorists were killed and one was arrested. All of the hostages were rescued, apart from one who was shot when the terrorists attempted to massacre the captives as the assault went in. The operation demonstrates the importance of continual training and effective rope work.

Military rappel seat

The military rappel seat is a relatively easy way of creating a rappel harness out of rope if a pre-fabricated webbing harness is not available.

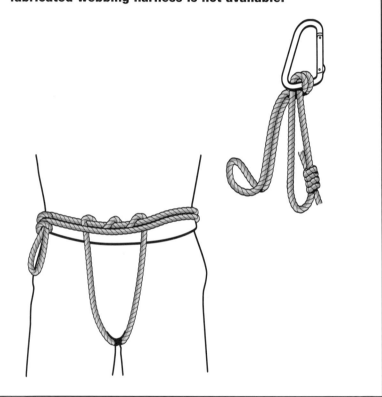

the person's chest and tied with a bowline.

The roper then takes the working end of the rope and pulls it out to arm's length. A figure-of-eight loop is tied at the end of the rope, and a karabiner is attached to a separate D-ring on the SPIE rope from the safety harness and the figure-of-eight loop is inserted.

Fast-roping

Elite units and special forces often use the fast-roping technique for quick insertion from a helicopter into an operational area. The technique is less complex than rappelling, but it also potentially hazardous as there is no safety line.

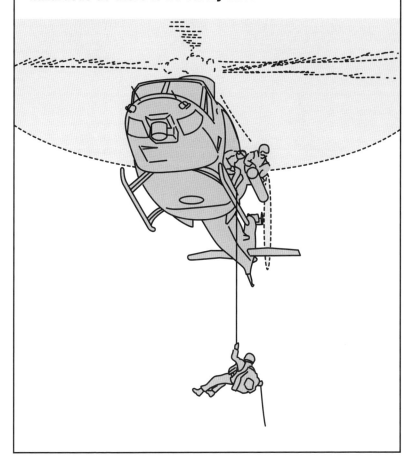

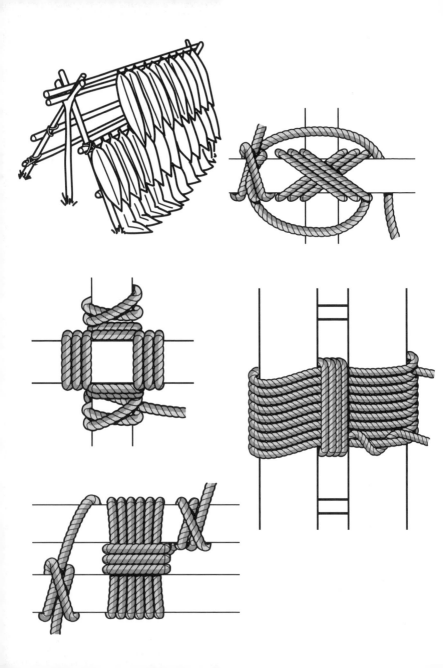

Raft construction is often used as a team-building and adventure activity by organizations such as the Scouts and by a range of outward bound and adventure groups. As far as the military is concerned, raft building is a part of survival training. A raft may provide the best means of travelling down a river to find safety after soldiers have been separated from their unit or airmen have crashed behind enemy lines. However, a raft can prove to be a dangerous hazard in itself if it is not constructed securely, especially if it has to travel over rapids.

In a survival situation, adequate supplies of good strong rope may not be available, in which case – if the location is a jungle environment – lianas, vines and other natural material can be used. Elsewhere, other forms of rope will need to be found in nature.

Log Raft

This is a simple but effective form of raft and it can be made entirely from natural materials in an extreme survival scenario, or with man-made ropes if available. The successful

....

Lashings are a particularly useful type of knot for practical building tasks. These include square, round and shear lashings, each of which is suited to a particular task.

3

Ropes and knots are essential for building a range of rafts and shelters in survival, recreational or military situations.

Using Ropes to Build Rafts and Shelters

Log raft

A log raft is a typical example of where ropes and knots may be used in a survival context. In these circumstances, however, the ideal type of rope may not be available, so alternatives such as jungle lianas can be utilized.

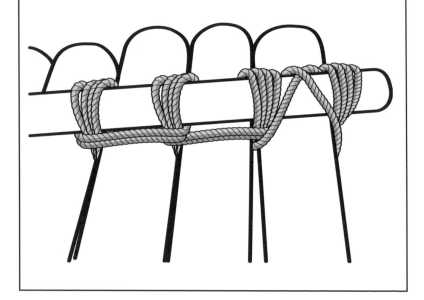

construction of a log raft requires the availability of a saw and a knife to cut and shape the logs.

Before starting the construction of the raft, it is a good idea to float the cut logs in the water first to see what their natural flotation profile is. Mark the top of the log above the water for

future reference. Check that the logs have enough buoyancy to keep at least half of the log out of the water. If a log is sinking too low and looks heavy in the water, cut a fresh one.

You will need to cut at least four cross bars to go under and over the logs. The cross bars should be cut to a length whereby they extend beyond the width of all of the logs put together.

Take some rope, or the best available natural equivalent, and cut some notches on the end of the crossbars so that the rope will not slip off them. Either a shear lashing or a round lashing can be used to tie the pressure bars together (see below). If it is possible, push boards down between the logs to act as a keel.

A-frame for steering oar

An A-frame mounted at the rear of the raft will hold the vessel's steering system. For this you will need two sturdy poles, a long steering pole and a flat piece of wood to act as a rudder.

Cut equally spaced holes into two logs at the back of the raft and insert the two poles, binding them together with a sheer lashing. Use another sheer lashing to lash the steering pole to the A-frame. Cut

A-frame for steering oar

The A-frame steering oar is a relatively simple construction that uses splayed poles joined by a shear lashing. The oar also has to pass through the lashing. Extra support is provided by guy lines.

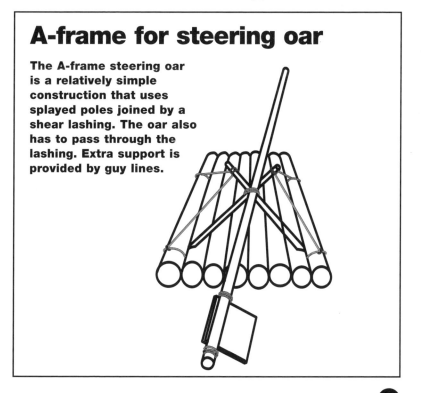

notches in the ends of the two cross poles and tie them with guy lines to the two outermost logs of the raft.

It may require some ingenuity to work out how to attach the steering blade to the base of the steering oar. If the steering oar is thick enough, you may be able to cut a hole wide enough for the steering blade to pass through. At the top of

the steering blade you could leave two wings, which are wider than the hole that the main part of the blade has passed through, and then lash the wings to the steering pole with round lashings. This should provide the best torsional strength and security for the oar.

Bamboo Raft

If you are in a tropical area, bamboo

Bamboo raft

The bamboo raft is another good example where either rope, twine or vines can be used to create a serviceable water-going vessel.

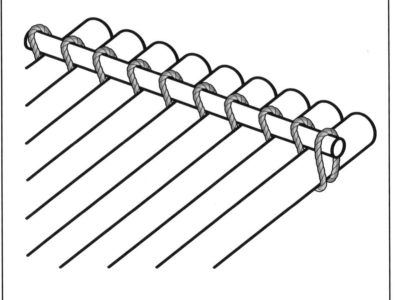

A-frame shelter

An A-frame shelter is a very useful construction that can be set up in almost any environment. Here lashings such as the sheer lashing are the best option for binding the structure together.

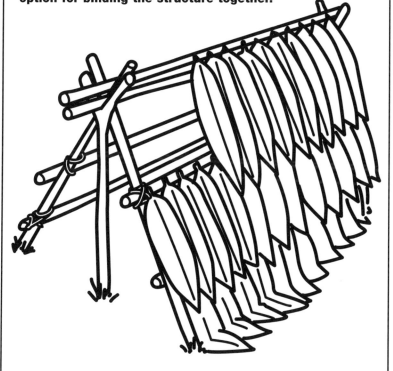

is an alternative to logs for the creation of a raft. Bamboo can be difficult to cut, so you will need a good saw, strong knife or machete, or alternatively burn the base of the bamboo poles until they fall.

Cut the bamboo to lengths of about 3m (10ft), and cut enough poles to provide sufficient width for the raft and to form two layers of bamboo, so as to raise the raft further out of the water.

Cut holes through all the pieces of bamboo in three places – near both ends and in the middle. These holes need to be large enough for a sturdy stake to pass through. Cut stakes which are somewhat longer than the overall width of the bamboos when put together. Then cut notches near the ends of the stakes to prevent rope slippage, and lash the ends of the stakes that have passed through both layers of the raft.

Tie the ends of the stakes together with either a shear lashing or a round lashing.

Shelters
A-frame shelter

A typical shelter that involves the use of lashings is the A-frame shelter. Cut suitably sized poles from saplings or the branches of larger trees and tie them together with a shear lashing. Depending on the time and resources you have available, you can create at least two and maybe four A-frames. Then take a long pole that will form the spine of the A-frame. Lash this to the A-frames with a diagonal lashing at each point, and then cover the whole structure with thick layers of vegetation.

Open lean-to shelter

This shelter can be constructed with a set of cut poles. You can lean one end of the top horizontal pole in the crook of a tree or lash it to a tree trunk. The other end can rest in the crook of an upright pole. Lean poles onto this supporting pole and attach with shear lashings. You can form a base with similarly lashed poles. The side poles can be cut to fit the descending diagonal of the side bars and also attached with shear lashings.

Lashings
Square lashing

For making rafts or shelters, a square lashing is a very useful knot to learn. The square lashing is ideal for binding two poles crossed at a 90-degree angle. To start the process, tie a clove hitch round the upright pole. Place the upright against a horizontal pole and then bind the rope behind the horizontal, in front of the top part of the vertical, and then pull tight. Continue with the rope over the lower part of the upright and then under the horizontal. Pull tight again and continue the process for about four turns.

To improve the strength of the lashing you can run 'frapping turns', which means taking the rope in front of the horizontal pole and behind the upper vertical pole.

Finish the process with another clove hitch on the right horizontal bar, or on the bottom vertical, pushed up close to the frapping turns. If there is any spare rope, tuck it under the lashing.

Open lean-to shelter

The open lean-to shelter is a very simple shelter that literally leans on something solid, like a tree. It requires secure lashings to support poles that are then covered with foliage. The sheer lashing is the best option for binding the structure together.

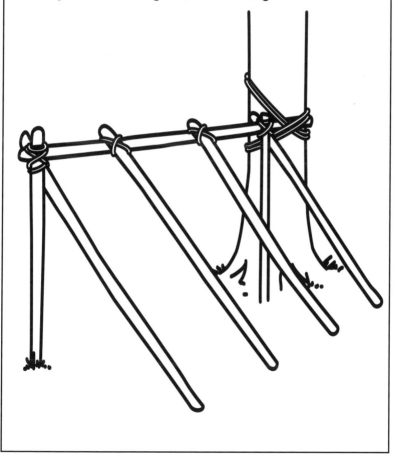

Diagonal lashing

The diagonal lashing is useful when, as the name implies, the poles to be tied do not cross at right angles. It is also handy when the poles need to be pulled towards each other to be tied.

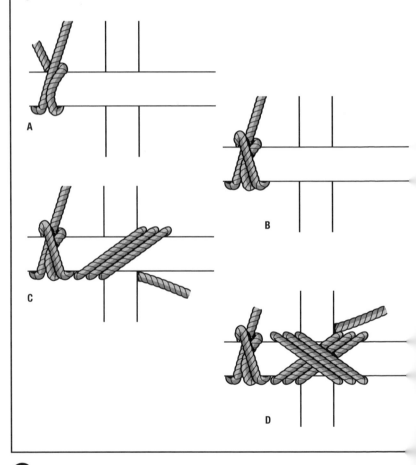

A

B

C

D

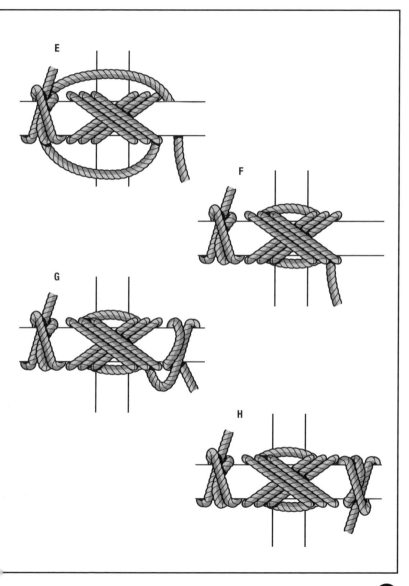

E

F

G

H

Square lashing

The square lashing is the essential knot for lashing poles or spars at right angles, and it provides a secure locking knot that will minimize movement and create optimal structural integrity.

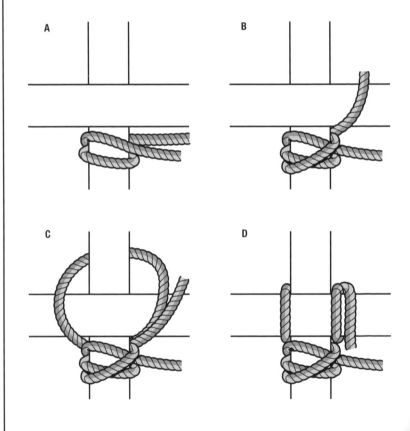

A

B

C

D

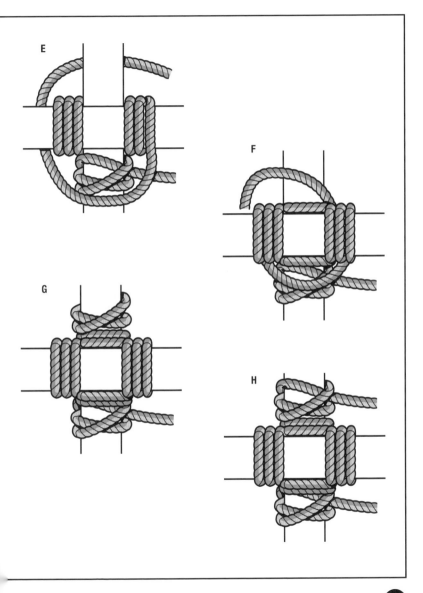

Round lashing

The round lashing can serve two purposes: either to lash two poles alongside each other or to create an extra length for a pole.

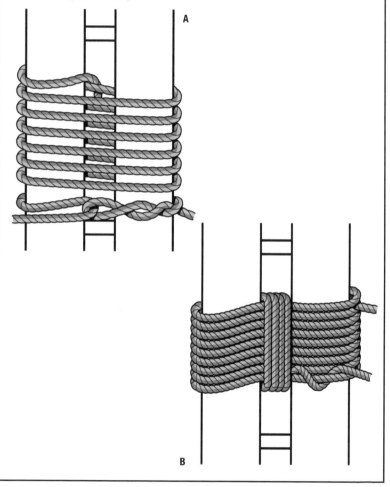

A

B

Timber hitch

The timber hitch is an ideal knot for pulling or towing pieces of timber, or any other cylindrical object that needs to be dragged along.

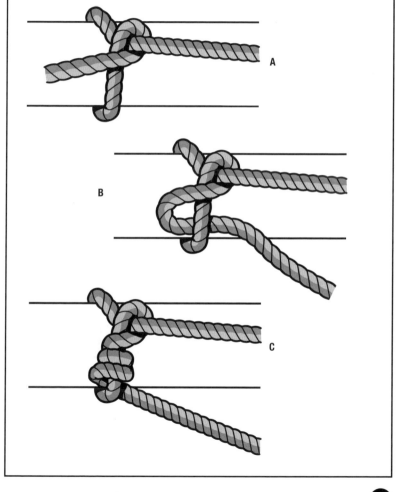

A

B

C

Round lashing

This lashing is used to lash two poles lying alongside each other. Begin with a clove hitch round both poles and then take the rope several times round the two poles. When you consider you have enough turns to secure the two pieces of wood, tie another clove hitch.

Diagonal lashing

This knot is used for bracing poles that are crossed and holding them firm.

Begin with a timber hitch horizontally across the two poles and pull it tight. Then take the working end round the back of the poles for several turns, first horizontally and then vertically. Each time you make a turn round the poles, pull it tight. Then make frapping turns behind then in front of each pole. Next tie a half hitch round one of the lower poles. Finish off with a clove hitch.

Sheer lashing

A sheer lashing can be used either to bind two poles lying parallel together or two poles that form splayed legs. If the poles are to be opened out and splayed, then the sheer lashing needs to be loose enough to allow this movement.

Start with a clove hitch round both poles lying parallel. Pull it tight then make a turn round the wood, trapping the end of the clove hitch

under the turn. Make a few turns before starting frapping turns down between the two poles and across the length of the turns that have been made. Once you have made two frapping turns, tie a half hitch and then finish with a clove hitch.

Timber hitch

The timber hitch can be used to tie a rope round a single log or bundle of timber for hauling. The real beauty of this knot is that the more it is pulled the tighter it gets.

Pass the working end behind the log or post and bring it round to the front. Now take the working end and pass it round the starting part. Then make a loop and take the working end between the standing end and itself. Carry on tucking the working end around itself to make two or more tucks. Then pull hard on the standing part to tighten the knot, ready for use.

Rolling hitch

The rolling hitch is an extension of the clove hitch and is often used to tie a knot to a pole, allowing the knot to be pulled from one direction. It can be doubled, however, so that the knot can be pulled from two directions.

The rope is put round the pole from front to back, bringing the working end up on the right side of the standing part. Then make a second turn round one pole and bring the working end between the diagonal that has been created and the standing part. Then make another turn. Tuck the working end under on the third turn. Pull on the working end and standing part to tighten.

Rolling hitch

The rolling hitch is used to secure a rope to a pole in such a way as to prevent its slipping. However, the rolling hitch is designed to work for only one direction of pull.

A

B

C

D

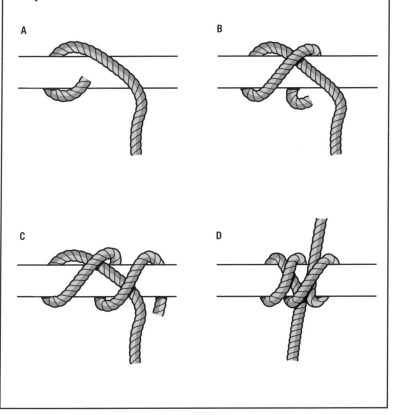

Sheer lashing

The sheer lashing is used for tying poles together where they might be splayed, for example in creating an A-frame or a tripod. The bindings should not be too tight if the poles are to be splayed.

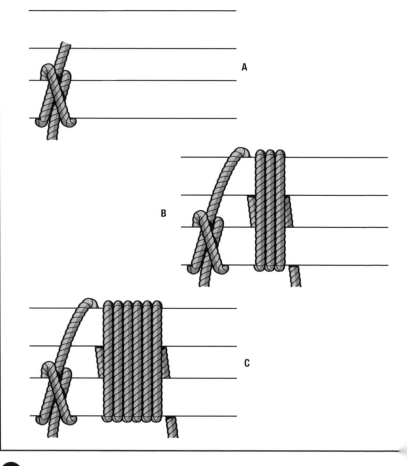

A

B

C

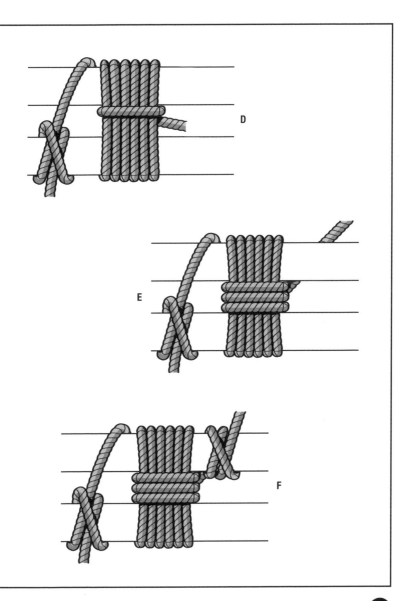

D

E

F

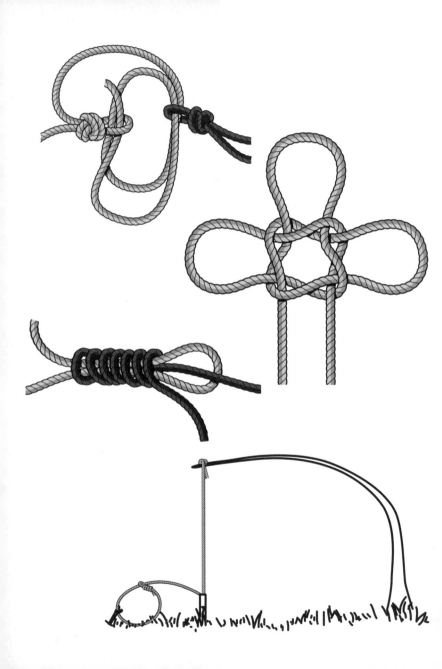

Knots have many practical uses and some have been created for specific ones: the Fireman's chair knot has practical uses as a rescue harness for emergency evacuation. The idea is that one loop should support the chest and arms and another loop support the legs under the knees. Two rope lengths extend at the top and bottom of the knot— one for lowering the patient and the other for guiding.

First create a bight in the rope and make a clockwise overhand loop. Then create a clockwise underhand loop and partly overlap the two loops, placing the right hand loop on top of the left. Take the leading edges of both loops and pull them sideways through the loops. Keep pulling the loops to tighten this part of the knot.

Take the left standing point and pass it round behind the left loop, then over the front and down in front of its own standing end. Pull it down to complete a half-hitch. Take the right standing part around the top of the right loop and back through its standing part.

Barrel sling

This knot has traditionally used for hoisting barrels and other cargo out

....

The more knots you know, the better chance you will have of coping in a survival situation where a rescue is required.

4

Knots and ropes are essential tools when setting traps, arranging fishing lines and for rescue techniques.

Useful Knots for Rescue, Fishing and Trapping

Fireman's chair knot

The fireman's chair knot is a particularly useful knot for rescue personnel to create a rescue sling – one loop is placed under the arms and the other is positioned under the legs.

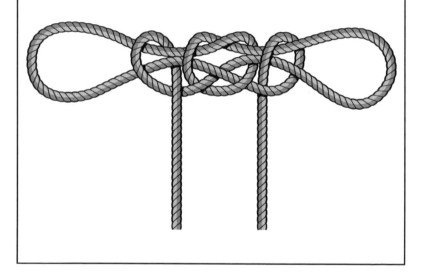

of the holds of ships. It would probably not meet modern health and safety requirements, and care should be taken not to stand beneath a heavy object that is being lifted by this method.

First pass the rope beneath the object, bring it around to the top and tie a half knot. Then separate the half knot and take the ring so formed

down the side of the object before pulling the knot tight on both sides. Tie a bowline to the standing part.

Plank sling

This sling can be used to suspend a plank of wood, and is therefore useful for creating a platform. First pass the rope under the plank and then form a bight in the standing part, which is

Barrel sling

The barrel sling is a very handy knot for suspending an object, though it should be noted that the barrel sling is designed for an objects on its sides, while a barrel hitch keeps it vertical.

Plank sling

This is an extremely useful sling for any situation where it is necessary to form a platform. It is simple to use once learned.

A

B

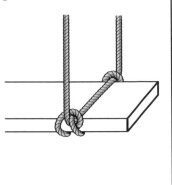

pushed through under the plank as well. Bring the working end back over the top of the plank and pass it through the bight. Take the other working end over across the plank in the opposite direction and pass it through that bight. Pull up the bights on both sides of the plank evenly, then tie the two ends together.

Three-way sheet bend

This handy knot is somewhat unusual and is used in those circumstances where three lines need to be tied together securely. First lay all the lines alongside each other and then

make a bight in one of the lines, whichever is the widest. Now take the working ends of the other two lines and pass them through the bight that you have formed in the first line. Then take each of the lines around the bight and pass them beneath their own standing part.

Chain-stitch lashing

This form of lashing is both effective and decorative and can be undone quickly. To begin, tie a fixed loop in one end of the line and then pass a bight from the standing part through it. Now take the working end around

Three-way sheet bend

Whereas most knots involve one or two ropes or lines, the three-way sheet bend is used for joining three lines.

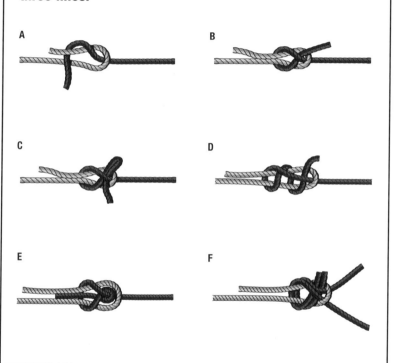

the parcel and then create another bight from the standing part, which is pulled through the bight. Take the working end around the parcel again and pull another bight from the standing part through the second bight. Repeat this process for as

long as necessary, depending on the size of the package and the length of the rope.

Diamond hitch knot
This is a useful knot for carrying loads of all shapes and sizes, as well

as attaching to hooks. (If you do not have this a hook with you, try making one from thorns, a nail or pin, or even sharp pieces of wood.

Hunting and Trapping Devices

Fishing
This method of fishing allows a line to do the work while you get some rest. Create a long line and hang hooks from it on other pieces of line. Attach one end of the main line to a post or tree trunk and tie a weight on to the other end of the line. Throw the weight into the water so that the line is stretched out diagonally.

If you can reach both sides of the river bank, an alternative is to attach the line to posts on either side of the bank and let the fishing lines and hooks hang in the water from that.

Chain stitch lashing

The chain-stitch lashing is useful for securing soft bundles such as sails or carpets which can easily fall out of conventional lashings.

DETAIL OF KNOTS

Diamond hitch

The Diamond Hitch has been used for many years to secure sometimes awkward loads on either a pack animal or a truck.

A

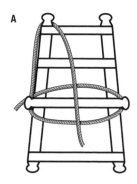

B

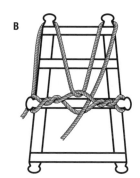

C

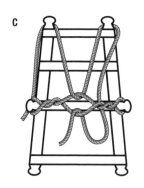

D

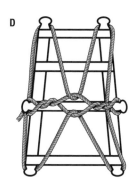

Versatackle

The versatackle is an extremely useful knot for creating the effect of a block and tackle, and can be used for towing or pulling a vehicle (or similar burden) out of a ditch. When the knot is under strain, care must be taken not to create too much friction.

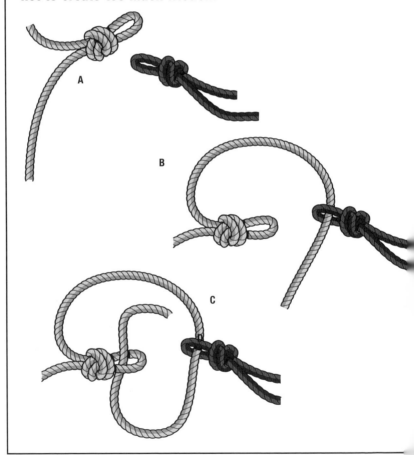

If you have a float, you can fish using a rod and line, with the hook hanging below the float. You can make your own fishing rod by cutting a suitably sized pole and tying a line and hook on to this. Ideally you need to cut a young branch that has some flexibility in it, otherwise a dry, stiff pole may well break under use.

If you are feeling adventurous you can try a spot of survival fly fishing. This method involves flicking an improvised 'fly' onto the surface of the water, with a hook embedded into the fly. This idea is that the fish will try to swallow the fly and take the hook as well. As fish are wary, the fly will need to be quite convincing, and may be made out of feathers or even a real insect.

Netting and basket traps

Another way of using rope, line and knots for survival is by creating nets to catch fish. A gill net can be created by tying lengths of rope horizontally between two trees and then tying vertical lines into the horizontal strands to create a grid. Look at the relevant knots for doing this, such as the ground line knot (p.131), which is specifically designed for tying a line to another line.

A more elaborate form of fish trap is a basket trap. This could take some time to construct and will require a lot of flexible pieces of wood, which can be bent around and tied to create a basket effect (see picture on p.122).

Eight-strand square plait braid

The braiding or plaiting of a rope is a traditional method of making it stronger. It also makes the rope easier to coil without tangling.

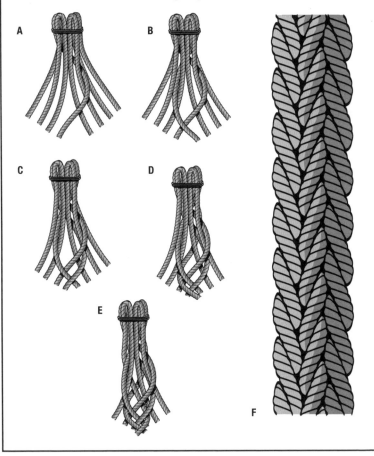

A

B

C

D

E

F

Nightline

A nightline can be an extremely effective way of catching fish while you busy yourself with other tasks or catch up with sleep.

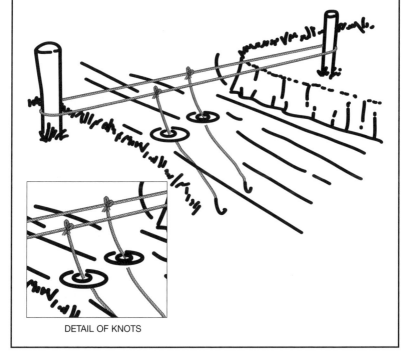

DETAIL OF KNOTS

Animal snare

Rope or string can be used to make a number of effective animal snares and traps for outdoor survival. One of the simplest snares involves first creating a loop in one end of a piece of wire or string; the other end is then anchored to a tree or post. You will need to attach the rope firmly to the anchor and create a loop around the standing part of the snare (see p.123). In order for the animal to put its head through the loop, you need to judge the size of the animal (for example, a rabbit) and place the loop at the right level with the optimum size of loop from

Basket trap

Although a basket trap can take a long time to make, it is an effective way of catching fish if placed in the right part of a river. As with netting, it should be used for a short period only, and never left indefinitely.

the ground. Try to ensure that the head goes through, but not the body. If necessary, you can support the loop off the ground with twigs. Place the loop in the centre of an obvious animal run, which you can identify by flattened grass and animal droppings. Make sure you camouflage the loop and the rope effectively.

Spring snare

This is a more complex snare system, which is created using the natural tension in a bent sapling or branch. You will need to tie a rope very securely to the top part of the sapling (see p.124) and then tie the other end to a hooking device. Cut an upward indentation into a piece of wood or a stump and bend the sapling over so that you can tether it with the hook. Then tie another, shorter rope to the hook, with a slip-knot noose at one end. The idea is that when the animal runs through the noose it will create a

Animal snare

A simple animal snare consists of either a wire or string loop that is designed to tighten once the animal's head is placed through it, resulting in the animal being either held or strangled.

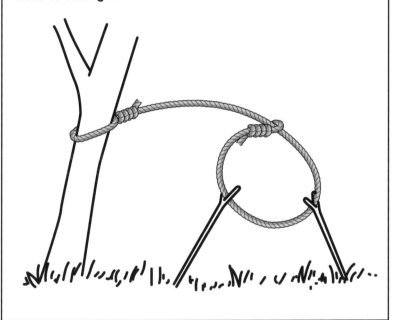

lateral drag on the retaining hook, which will release it. The sapling will then spring up, tightening the noose around the animal and lifting it off the ground.

If it is difficult to find a suitable sapling, a variation on the theme is a weighted branch. This involves binding either a stone or a heavy piece of wood on to one end of a branch and passing the non-weighted end through the V of a tree or a similar structure. Tie the snare system described above to the non-weighted end of the branch, with the weighted part suspended on the opposite side of the tree purely by the counterforce of the hook. The

Spring snare

A spring snare is an arrangement whereby an animal sets off a trigger device, which in turn releases tension in a bent branch or weighted pole and pulls a noose tight around the animals's neck.

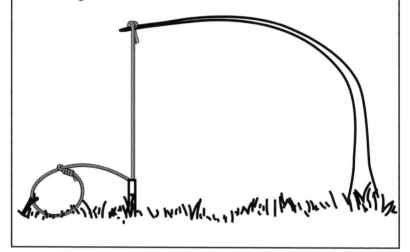

lateral drag of an animal running through the noose should trigger exactly the same result as is produced by a spring snare, as the weight is released and pulls the snared animal into the air.

Spear trap

This is quite a complex and perhaps somewhat ambitious means of killing prey. The basis of the trap is a flexible branch held under tension with a sharp pointed spear lashed on to its end. When the tension on the trap is

released, the branch whips around in an arc and plunges the spear into the animal. Take care only to build such traps well away from trails or paths frequented by humans. Always construct or inspect the trap from behind its 'killing zone'. Lash the thick end of the sapling either to a tree trunk or to some posts in the ground. At the other end of the sapling, lash one or more sharpened pieces of wood (see pp. 100–5 for suitable lashings). About 1m (3ft) from the end of the sapling, create a holding device,

Spear trap

A spear-trap involves a bent branch, held under tension and fitted with spear-like pieces of wood and a trigger device. The trap should be set up with extreme care and only from behind its arc of travel.

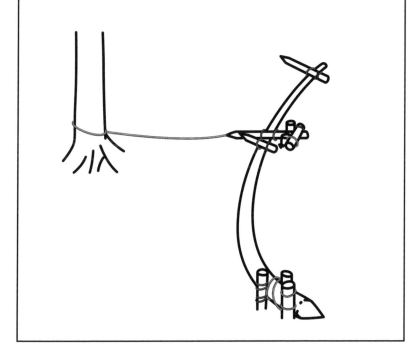

which may consist of two posts in the ground and a horizontal bar with a sharpened end pointing in the direction of the target area. One of the spears attached to the spring-loaded sapling can be attached to this protruding end via a loop, which is in turn attached to a rope leading across the animal track. The other end of this rope will be attached securely to a tree or post.

The idea is that when the animal walks into the line, the loop will slip off the end of the spear and release the tension on the sapling, which will whip towards the target. You will need, however, to judge carefully the amount of pressure in the sapling and the strength of the loop, otherwise the pressure of the sapling alone may release the loop.

Bird snares

Snares can be used to catch birds, if they are located along appropriate perching areas and are made of fine, light materials. See the illustration below for one such snare trap.

Other Useful Knots
Surgeon's knot

This knot is so called because it has traditionally been used by the medical profession to tie off blood vessels. Because it is a delicate knot

Bird snares

Catching birds is difficult, and bird snares should be made out of very light material such as horse hair or fishing line. The noose should run very easily if the bird enters it.

Surgeon's knot

The surgeon's knot is used in medical practice to tie a suture, and it is characterized by an extra twist in what would otherwise be a reef knot. It is also used in fly fishing and similar outdoor pursuits.

suited to binding slippery parts, it is also valued for other uses, such as tying knots in fishing line.

Begin by crossing over the two working ends of the line and tie a knot. As with the reef knot, it is important to know which way the knot has been tied in order to get the balance of the knot right. Take another turn and then cross the two working ends in the opposite way from the first. So if you put right over left to begin with, now put left over right. Now tie a half knot and tighten it up.

Blood knot

This knot is often used for joining thin lines of the same thickness and is therefore particularly useful for fishing line. The blood knot is secure under strain, but can be very difficult to untie.

Place the two lines side by side from opposite directions. Take the working end of the top line around one turn of the lower line. Carry on making several turns to bind the two lines securely. Then pass the working end between the two lines. Then repeat the process, using the working end of the bottom line, making the same number of turns and finishing by passing the working end between the two lines. When this sequence has been done, pull in opposite directions on the two different lines, which will bring the knots together.

Blood knot

The blood knot is usually tied in monofilament nylon line and is often used in fly fishing. It is a difficult knot to tie properly and it can jam easily, making it complicated to untie.

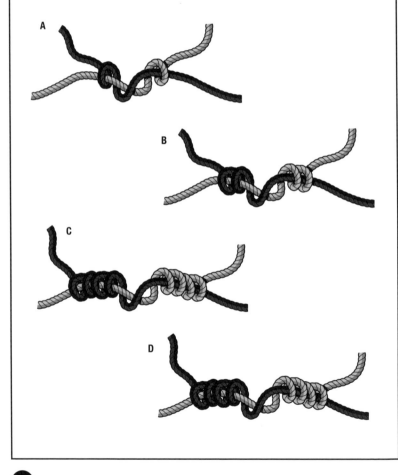

Linfit knot

This is a symmetrical knot primarily used for joining larger diameter fishing lines. It was created by an angler specifically for anglers.

Linfit knot

This knot was first devised by an angler, and it is designed for joining thicker lines together.

Start by creating bights at the end of two pieces of line and then place one across the other. Then take the working end of the top line around and under the bight of the lower lines, going from right to left. Then take the working end from the lower line from left to right across the bight. Take the left-hand working end in a clockwise way around the left standing part. Bring this working end through the left-hand bight. Then take the right-

hand working end the other way around the right-hand standing part. Next take this working end through the right-hand bight. By pulling on each working end and standing part you should be able to tighten up the knot so that it looks symmetrical.

Albright special

This knot is often used by anglers to join lines of different diameters. As the knot remains small on the original line, it can pass through rings and other devices without jamming. The knot should be tied carefully to minimize its volume.

Albright special

The Albright special is a useful knot for anglers who want to join two pieces of line in a very compact way. This can be achieved by carefully winding the loops so that they lie neatly next to each other.

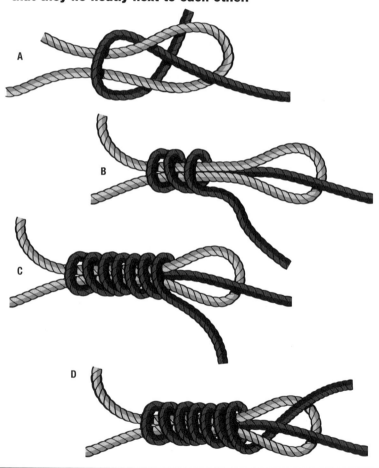

First make a bight in the thick line. Place the narrow line over the bight, then take the working end over one side of the bight. Now take the working end over the top of the bight and over the standing part, before wrapping it over and down between the legs of the bight. Then make another wrapping turn alongside the first one. Repeat as many wrapping turns as you think necessary to secure the knot and then pass the working end through the bight.

Groundline hitch

This knot is designed for hitching a thin piece of line to a thick one. It is thought to be even more secure than a clove hitch and less likely to jam.

Groundline hitch

The groundline hitch takes its name from the weighted groundline of a fishing net, but it is also used for a wide variety of other purposes in which a rope needs to be attached to a pole.

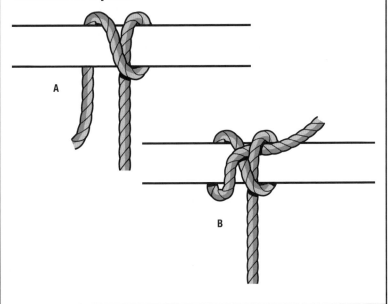

A

B

Half blood knot

The half blood knot can be used to tie fishing line to an object such as a lure or to a hook. It is relatively easy to tie and is also quite secure.

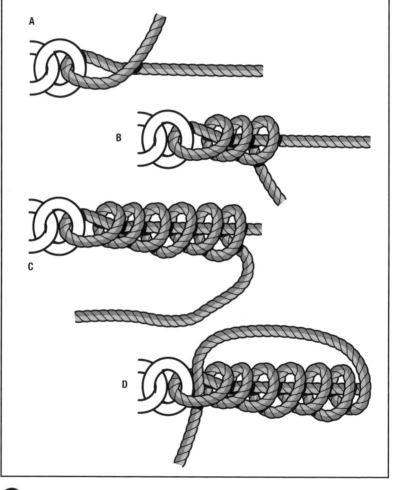

A

B

C

D

The knot name refers to the weighted ground line to which the net would be attached.

Take the working end of a thin line and move it over and around the back of a thicker line. Then take it back around to the left of its own standing part. Now take the working end diagonally across the front of the turn; take it around again until it is to the right of its own standing part. Grasp the top of the first turn and pull it upwards to create a bight. Then pass the end of the standing part through this bight and pull the standing part down to trap it.

Half blood knot

This knot is normally used for attaching a fishing line to a hook or to other equipment, such as lures.

Take the working end through the end of the hook or other attachment point. Twist the working end and standing part together, making at least five or six twists. This twisting should ensure tension is held on both parts of the line. Then bring the working end back again and take it through the original loop.

Palomar knot

This knot if often used by anglers to attach a bight to a hook, lure or other object, especially where the knot needs to withstand heavy strain.

Begin by taking the bight through the ring and then bring it around the standing part. Then take it around

and through the loop to create an overhand knot. Pull on the ring itself and the standing part to tighten.

Jansik special

This knot is used by anglers on occasions when the highest level of security is required.

Begin by taking the working end through the ring and then back around under its own standing part. Then take the end through the ring once again and under the standing part. Take the working end around the two previous turns and through the loop. Then make three or four turns before tightening the knot.

Turle knot

This is a well-known angler's knot which can be traced back to the nineteenth century.

Take the line through the eye of the hook or other attachment point and then take it around the hook shaft itself and across its own standing part. Then tie an overhand knot to finish.

True lover's knot

This knot is not as strong as many angling knots, but is often used to tie a line to a lure.

Begin by tying an overhand knot in the standing part of the line and then take the working end through the ring of the lure. Next take the other end back through the overhand knot. Then tie a second overhand knot,

Palomar knot

The Palomar knot is one of the strongest knots for tying a fishing line to a lure or a hook. It can also be used for other purposes in which a line or rope needs to be tied securely to an object, such as a clip.

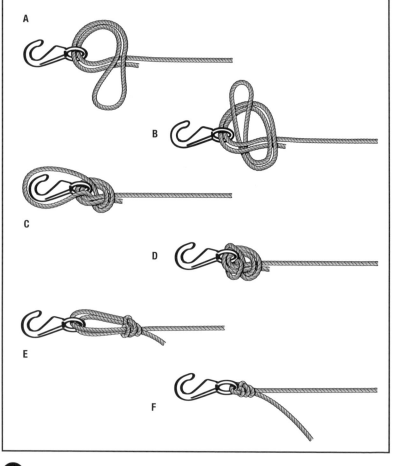

Jansik special

The Jansik special is a high-strength knot which is often used in fishing circles to tie a line to a hook. It incorporates three circles of line through the ring of the object for maximum security.

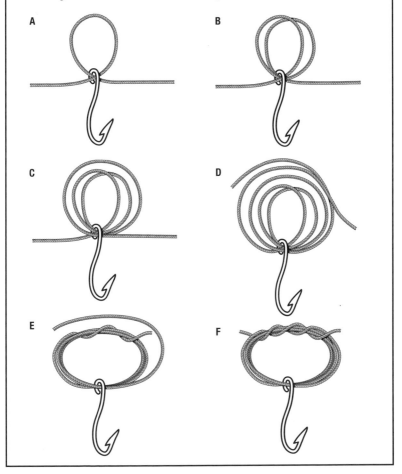

Turle knot

The Turle knot is named after Major William Greer Turle who fished in the chalk streams of Hampshire, England, in the nineteenth century. It is regarded as a highly reliable way of attaching a line to an eyed hook.

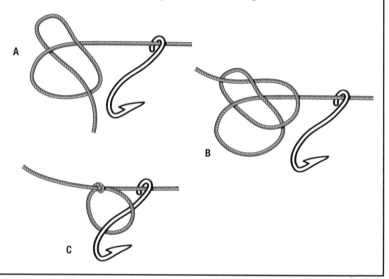

using the working end on the standing part of the line. Move the second knot close to the first and the pull on the standing part to tighten.

Spade-end knot

The spade end referred to in this knot's name is the shaft of an eyeless hook, which is splayed at the end to stop the line attached to it from slipping off. The knot can also be used for attaching a thin line to a thicker one. First create a loop in the thin line, bringing the working end alongside the thick line. Then take a side of the loop and wrap it around both its own strand and the other line. Make sure the turns are neatly arranged alongside each other. When the turns are complete, pass the end of the loop over the other line and pull on the standing part and the working end to tighten the knot.

True lover's knot

The true lover's knot is not so much a knot in itself, but more of a variation on a theme, the underlying imagery being that of two people joined by love. The knot can be created out of two interlocked overhand knots.

Clinch knot

This knot is often used for attaching a line to a hook. First take the working end twice through the eye of the hook and make a round turn. Then take the working end around the standing part for five or six turns. Then take the working end and push it through the first round turn. To finish, pull on both the hook and the standing part. Keep the turns neatly near to the eye of the hook.

Double overhand loop

This knot is made from doubled line and can be particularly useful tied in fishing line. Once you have made a bight at the end of a doubled piece of line, tie an overhand knot with a generous eye in the knot. Then pass the bight over the overhand knot and take it through the knot's eye. In order to tighten the knot, pull on the bight. This knot can be difficult to untie once it has been placed under strain.

Spade-end knot

The spade-end knot is a reliable knot for attaching a line to the spade-end type of hook where there is no obvious security from the eye of a conventional hook.

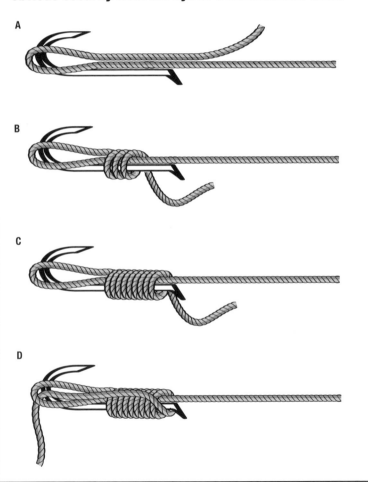

A

B

C

D

Clinch knot

The clinch knot is another very reliable knot for attaching a line to a lure or to a hook where there needs to be a guarantee that the two will not separate.

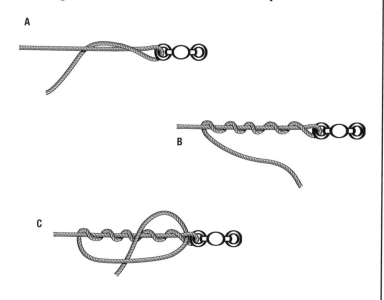

Double overhand sliding loop

This knot is often used by anglers to tie a line to a hook or similar object. Take the working end of the line behind the standing part to create a crossing turn. Then take the working end around the crossing turn twice. Now push the working end through the two turns. Pull on the working end and the loop to tighten the knot.

Englishman's loop

The loop formed by this knot can be useful for a number of purposes and is often used by anglers.

First create a slipped overhand knot and then pass a bight through a crossing turn to create the first overhand knot. Next take the working end over the standing part and around itself, pulling it under the turn to create the second overhand knot.

Double overhand loop

The double overhand loop is considered to be a simple and relatively reliable knot that can be used in fishing, and other applications, where maximum strength is not required.

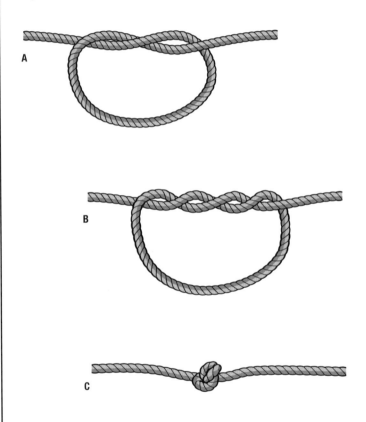

A

B

C

Double overhand sliding loop

This is one of a variety of ways of attaching a fishing line to either a hook, a lure or another object.

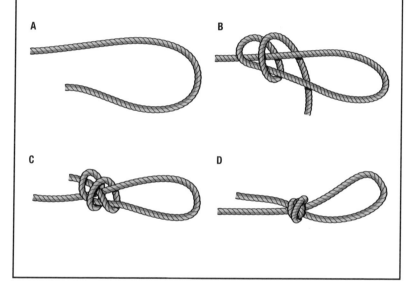

A   B

C   D

Then pull on the standing part and the loop to tighten the knot.

Blood-dropper knot

Related to the blood knot described earlier, this knot is used on a fishing line to create a loop, which can be put to various purposes. First tie a loose overhand knot and take the working end over and then under the standing part. Then take the working end around the standing part at least five times. Pull out the centre of the simple line through the central twist to create a loop. To tighten the knot, pull on the line on each side of the twists.

Bimini twist

This knot is exceptional for the fact that, unlike most knots, it does not weaken the line in which it was made. When the knot is complete, it

Englishman's loop

This knot was mostly used by anglers, though it has lost some favour now because it does not tie so securely in nylon rope.

creates a loop at the end of the line; the loop is made secure by the friction of the various twists behind it.

To begin, take about 1.5m (5ft) of line and fold it back to create a loop. Hold the two pieces of line together, leaving about 45cm (18in) of working end. Then make twists by turning the loop. You can make approximately 20 twists for optimum reliable strength.

While holding the working end and standing part, someone else should pull the loop strands apart to force the twists to tighten. The working end should be rolled around the twists as they tighten. Once the working end has passed around all the twists it can be taken around one strand of the loop and a half

hitch tied. Then take the working end around both lines of the loop. It should then be taken under itself twice. The working end is now pulled tight.

Blood-dropper knot

The blood-dropper knot is often used in fishing to attach a lure or some other object above a jig, or to attach a second fly to the leader.

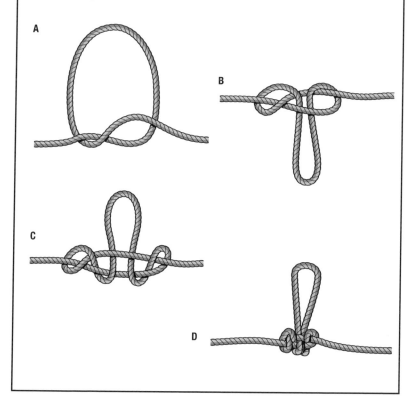

A

B

C

D

Bimini twist

Bimini twist: this is perhaps the strongest of all fishing knots and it does not weaken the line in which it is tied. Because of its strength, it is used in sport fishing, where heavy strains are encountered.

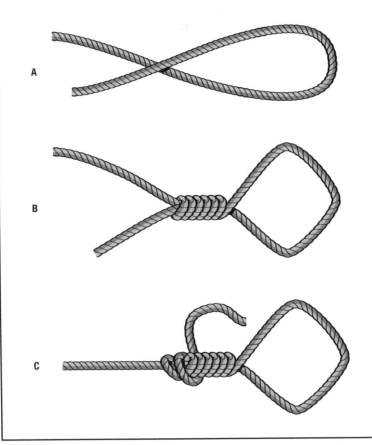

A

B

C

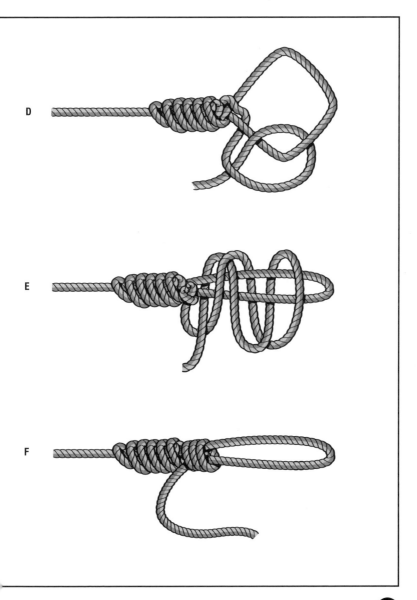

D

E

F

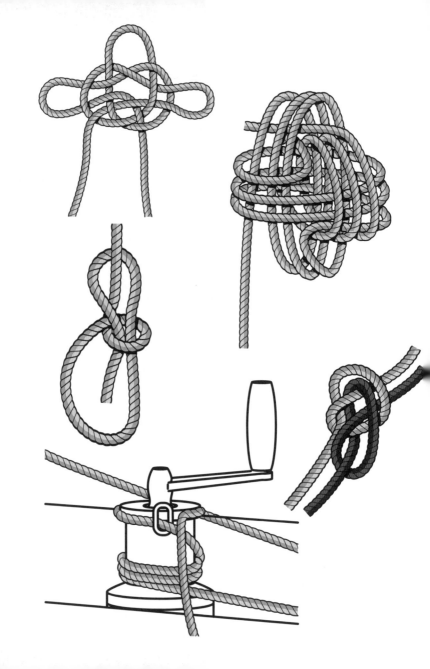

Ropes and lines have been used at sea for as long as sails have existed as maritime propulsion. The ancient Egyptians mainly used oars to move their boats up and down the Nile, but they also relied on sails for those occasions where there was a following wind. Sometimes they went beyond the confines of the Nile to places as far afield as Crete and Palestine. Apart from using ropes to haul the sails, the Egyptians also sometimes used a massive twisted rope that was attached to the bow and the stern and literally kept the boat together by providing tension. There is some evidence to show that ropes were also used to provide structural support for the sides of the boat.

The Minoans and the Phoenicians were also great maritime peoples, and the Greeks are likely to have learnt about constructing their successful triremes from the Phoenicians. The Greek trireme was central to the success of Athens as a civilization and as a military/naval power. Its main power came from about 170 oars, but it also had two

....

Sailors will often employ certain key knots such as the bowline and figure-of-eight. The use of blocks, tackle and winches all demand a good working knowledge of ropes and knots.

5

The correct use of ropes, lines and knots is essential for safe and efficient seamanship.

Using Ropes and Lines at Sea

Ancient Egyptian boat

The Egyptians developed the technique of using a massive rope to maintain the structural integrity of a boat. Ropes were also used as rigging for boats that travelled on longer distances.

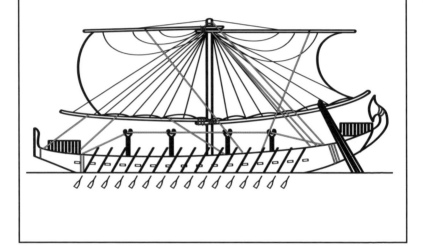

masts—a mainmast and a foremast, with square sails. The sails were only used for cruising, and in battle the mast was lowered and the ship was entirely dependent on its oarsmen. There is some evidence that there may have been an emergency rig designed to get the boat out of trouble, but the main rig would also have been used for this purpose when it was required.

The ships used by Rome were similar to the Greek triremes and their crews used similar tactics in combat, such as ramming. The Byzantines developed lighter craft, which sometimes had as many as three masts. Another Mediterranean innovation was the triangular sail. Over time, the important naval change was that the sails remained up during action. This meant that

Greek trireme

The Greek trireme typically carried a mast, rigging and sail that could be taken down quickly when the ship was cleared for action. The sail was used only for cruising.

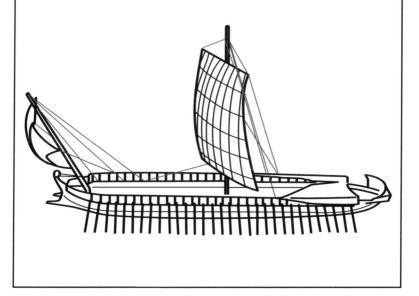

the rigging of the ship was now recognized as a tactical system rather than an optional extra.

In Northern Europe the earliest Viking ships (eighth century) probably relied entirely on oars and would have had no rigging. Such boats would likely have sailed on inshore waters only, and sails and rigging would probably have been considered to be more of an

encumbrance than a help. Likewise, in England evidence from a ship unearthed at Sutton Hoo shows that this was entirely dependent on oars.

Developments in ship building
As time went on, however, Norse ships with masts became more common. Typically a 12m (40ft) mast was installed with a square sail. This would have helped the Viking ships

Viking ship

A Viking ship would have relied heavily on oar propulsion, especially in coastal waters, but sails were used when expeditions went farther afield, such as forays to Britain and the Continent.

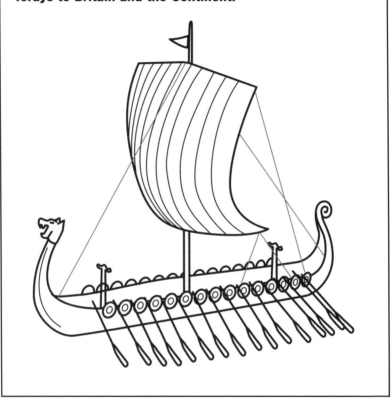

to sail across the North Sea, to conduct raids on England, and further down the English Channel to raid France and beyond to Spain and Portugal.

Some Norse invaders settled in Normandy and when William the Conqueror invaded England in 1066, his army was carried in boats similar to those used by the Vikings. Evidence from the Bayeux Tapestry shows that by 1066 rigging had become more sophisticated. There was a stay and backstay, as well as shrouds. It is significant to note that the sail and the rest of the rigging were now the main form of propulsion while the oars were secondary. The modern fighting sail ship, supreme until the invention of steam power, had arrived.

Over time, the number of masts increased, to include the foremast, mainmast, mizzen-mast, and eventually (on larger vessels) fourth

Norman ship

The Norman ships depicted in the Bayeux Tapestry show that sails had in the eleventh century become the main means of propulsion.

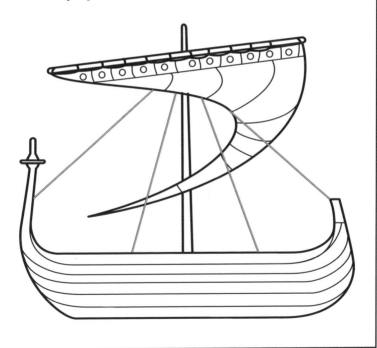

Caravel

The caravel with its lateen sail was used widely by the Portuguese in the early voyages of discovery. It was a highly efficient system of rigging, which enabled the exploration of inshore waters and the ability to sail against the wind.

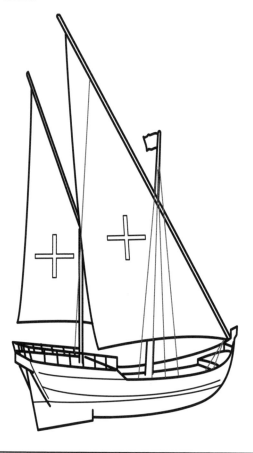

and fifth masts. The rigging also became ever more complex. Ungainly high-sided vessels were gradually replaced by more seaworthy and manoeuvrable ships in England. In the Mediterranean, the rowed galley remained in use for a long time, especially by the Venetians. Eventually, masts and sails were introduced and a hybrid craft came into being, known as a galleass. The galley design would influence English shipbuilders so that HMS *Revenge*, the flagship of Sir Francis Drake at the battle against the Spanish Armada in 1588, was described as 'race-built, like a galleass.' It was also influenced by the design of the Portuguese caravel. This layout of boat was inspired by Portuguese fishing vessels and was used by Prince Henry the Navigator for the ships he deployed for the famous early voyages of discovery, which included the exploration of the coast of Africa, the route to India via the Cape of Good Hope and also, by extension, the journey to America by Columbus. The Arab name for a caravel-type boat was *qarib*, though there is now some discussion as to whether the caravel with the lateen sail was really brought to Western Europe by the Moorish invaders or whether it had already existed in the Mediterranean region. Whatever its genesis, the lateen-rigged caravel was highly manoeuvrable, relatively cheap to construct and became

popular with ship builders in Northern Europe.

The advantage of the lateen sail was that the ship could sail much closer to the wind than could a square sail. This ability gave the Portuguese an advantage when exploring inshore waters on the African coast, getting them out of danger if attacked and sailing home against the wind. The lateen-sail caravel would influence the design of the Bermuda sloop, which in turn was the inspiration for the modern yacht.

Further developments

By the late seventeenth century, the rigging of ships was still rather rudimentary, and could not be trimmed very easily. However, smaller craft, such as frigates and sloops, were faster, more seaworthy and more efficient.

In the nineteenth century, a typical British ship was the '74'. This had three masts—the mainmast, foremast and mizzen-mast. There was also a bowsprit at the bows of the ship, which was used partly to brace the mainmast and partly to act as anchor for the forestays. There was a variety of sails, including the lower sail, topsail, topgallant and loyal. The masts were built in sections, and where the mainmast met the topmast there were trestletrees and tops. From these, shrouds supported the topmast.

Old sailing lore

SHROUDS, (haubans, Fr. scrud, Sax.) a range of large ropes extended from the mast-heads to the right and left side of the ship, to support the masts, and enable them to carry sail, &c.

The shrouds are always divided into pairs or couples: that is to say, one piece of rope is doubled ... and the two parts fastened together at a small distance from the middle, so as to leave a sort of noose or collar to fix upon the mast-head. This collar being fixed in its place, close down upon the trestle-trees ... a pair of shrouds depend from it, whose lower ends ought to reach down to the deck. The lower ends of these shrouds are set up or extended to the channel ... on the outside of the ship, by the application of mechanical powers, as explained in the articles dead-eye and laniard.

The shrouds as well as the sails are denominated from the masts to which they belong. Thus they are the main, fore, and mizen shrouds, the main top-mast, fore-top-mast, or mizen top-mast shrouds, and the main topgallant, fore top-gallant, or mizen top-gallant shrouds.

The number of shrouds by which a mast is sustained, as well as the size of rope of which they are formed, is always in proportion to the size of the mast, and the weight of sail it is intended to carry.

The two foremost shrouds on the starboard and larboard side of the ship are always fitted first upon the mast-head and then the second on the starboard and the second on the larboard, and so on till the whole number is fixed. The intention of this arrangement is to brace the yards with greater facility when the sails are close-hauled, which could not be performed without great difficulty if the foremost shrouds were last fitted on the mast-head, because the angle which they would make with the mast would then be greatly increased. See also SWIFTER.

The topmast-shrouds are extended from the topmast heads to the edges of the tops ... The lower dead-eye, employed for this purpose, is fitted with an iron band, called the foot-hook-plate, which passes thro' a hole in the edge of the top, and communicates with a rope called the foot-hook shroud, whose lower end is attached to the shrouds of the lower mast ... The upper ends of the foot-hook shrouds are furnished with an iron hook, which enters a hole in the lower end of the foot-hook plate, so that when the top-mast shrouds are extended to secure the mast, the foot-hook shrouds necessarily acquire an equal tension by means of the foot-hook plate, which, passing through the top, transmits the effort of the mechanical powers to the foot-hook shrouds below.

William Falconer's *Dictionary of the Marine*

Old sailing lore

STAYS. Strong ropes, to support the masts forward, which extend from their upper part, at the mast-head, toward the fore part of the ship. The stays are denominated from the masts, lower-stays, topmast-stays, topgallant-stays, flagstaff or royal stays, &c.

The Elements and Practice of Rigging and Seamanship

A large amount of rigging was involved, usually made from rope made in the yards of the navy. Forward from the mast, the rigging was known as forestays, whereas behind the mast it was known as shrouds. Each mast had its own shrouds. There were shrouds for the main topmast, fore-topmast, mizzen topmast, main topgallant, fore-topgallant and mizzen topgallant. Lanyards and blocks were used to apply tension to the shrouds.

Running rigging included braces, sheets, haliards, clue-lines and brails. The sails, which included the main-sail, fore-sail, mizzen, main-stay-sail, forestay and mizzen-stay-sail, were hauled into position by lines. When the sail was furled, it was attached to

74 ship

The 74 was the standard two-decked fighting ship of the British Royal Navy, and carried 74 guns. These ships had three masts and elaborate rigging.

horizontal pieces of timber known as yards by ropes known as gaskets. The furling and unfurling of sails was carried out by experienced seamen known as topmen, who had to do this job in all weathers.

The Modern Yacht

Yacht design has been developing since the seventeenth century. Charles II, inspired by what he had seen of Dutch yachts, or *jaghts*, while in exile in the Netherlands, had two yachts built for himself and his brother the Duke of York, and raced them from Greenwich to Gravesend and back again. In 1851 the schooner *America* won a race round the Isle of Wight organized by the British Royal Yacht Squadron. The trophy was then named the Americas Cup, which continues today.

In 1893 the yacht *Britannia* was built for the Prince of Wales and became one of the most successful yachts ever built. Intrepid single-handed feats of sailing were performed by Joshua Slocum, who sailed around the world alone in 1895–98, Sir Francis Chichester, who in 1960 won the first single-handed transatlantic race, and Robin Knox-Johnston, who won the first round-the-world single-handed yacht race in 1969.

There is nothing like competition to improve design efficiency. Once the US schooner *America* had beaten the British, they knew it was time to go

> # Old sailing lore
>
> **CRINGLES.** Small loops made on the bolt-rope of a sail; used to fasten different ropes to, hook the reef tackles to, for drawing the sail up to its yard, to fasten the bridles of the bowline to, and to extend the leech of the sail, &c.
>
> *The Elements and Practice of Rigging and Seamanship*

back to the drawing board and do some serious re-design, which extended from the hull to the sails and rigging. Later an International Rule was introduced in 1906, and revised in 1919, that made racing a fairer sport.

The types of yacht used today can broadly be divided as sloops, ketches and cutters. Of these, the sloop is the simplest form, usually having one mast. Its history goes back to the seventeenth century, when it was developed in Bermuda by a Dutchman. The Dutch in turn had been influenced by the Spanish, who once ruled the Netherlands, and the Spanish in turn had been

Old sailing lore

RIGGING, a general name given to all the ropes employed to support the mast; and to extend or reduce the sails, or arrange them to the disposition of the wind.

The former, which are used to sustain the masts, remain usually in a fixed position, and are called standing rigging; such are the shrouds, stays, and back-stays. The latter, whose office is to manage the sails, by communicating with various blocks, or pullies, situated in different places of the masts, yards, shrouds, &c. are comprehended in the general term of running-rigging. Such are the braces, sheets, haliards, clue-lines, brails, &c.

In rigging a mast, the first thing usually fixed upon its head, is a circular wreath or rope, called the grommet, or collar, which is firmly beat down upon the top of the bounds. The intent of this is to prevent the shrouds from being fretted or worn by the trestle-trees, or shoulders of the mast; after this are laid on the two pendents, from whose lower ends the main, or fore-tackles are suspended and next, the shrouds of the starboard and larboard side, in pairs, alternately. The whole is covered by the stays, which are the largest ropes of the rigging.

When a yard is to be rigged, a grommet is also driven first on each of its extremities: next to this are fitted on the horses, the braces; and, lastly, the lifts, or top-sail sheet-blocks: all of which are explained in their proper places.

The principal objects to be considered in rigging a ship appear to be strength, convenience, and simplicity; or the properties of affording sufficient security to the mast, yards, and sails; of arranging the whole machinery in the most advantageous manner, to sustain the masts, and facilitate the management of the sails; and of avoiding perplexity, and rejecting whatever is superfluous or unnecessary. The persection of this art then consists in retaining all those qualities, and in preserving a judicious medium between them.

William Falconer's *Dictionary of the Marine*

HMY *Britannia*

His Majesty's Yacht *Britannia* was a large gaff-rigged cutter that won most of the races it was sailed in. When King George V died, he asked for his yacht to be sunk.

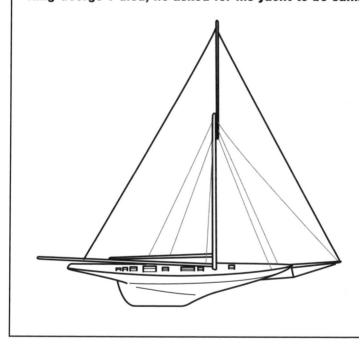

influenced by their Moorish invaders, who had introduced the lateen sail, as used on the Arab *dhow*.

Soon these Bermuda sloops began to make their mark. Their speed and agility made them attractive for a wide range of users. They were used by forces fighting for independence in America and also by pirates. The

British themselves did not take long to recognize their value, and began to commission their own well-armed Bermuda sloops. These sloops were often used for rapid communications and one, HMS *Pickle*, carried the news to England of the British victory at Trafalgar, as well as the death of Admiral Lord Nelson, in 1805.

Bermuda rigged sloop

**The Bermuda rigged sloop is the standard pattern for
many yachts today. It was developed from a design of
yachts that originated with a Dutch ship designer based
in Bermuda. It is normally single-masted.**

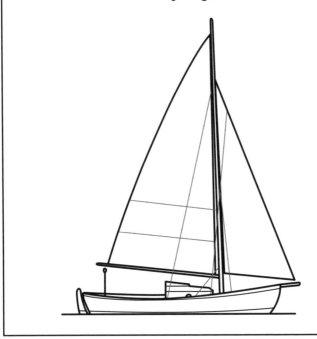

The modern Bermuda rigged sloop
normally has two triangular sails
consisting of a main-sail and fore-
sail. The leading edge of the main-
sail is attached to the mast and it
keeps its shape by being attached to
a swivelling boom. The fore-sail is
attached to the forestay and two
sheets are attached to the corner and
are led down each side of the boat.
An additional sail, also known as a
spinnaker, can be raised when sailing
with the wind. This has a sheet
attached to one bottom corner and a
guy line and a pole attached to the
other.

In modern boats the shrouds that support the mast are often made from wire. There is normally a forestay and a backstay as well as lateral shrouds, all of which provide optimum tension on the mast at all angles. The tension can be adjusted with screws.

The rigging on a boat is divided between halyards, sheets and control lines. The halyard is used to raise the head of the sail and control the luff (the leading edge of the sail). Originally halyards were made of manila or hemp rope. On a Bermuda rig there is one halyard. The halyard is attached either by a shackle, a bowline or by a half-hitch with a figure-of-eight knot. The halyard can be used to raise the sail conventionally or by other means, such as 'jumping' the halyard. This involves one member of the crew jumping up and grabbing the halyard from a higher point than normal. On a modern yacht, the halyard often runs inside the mast and emerges onto a winch from which it can be adjusted.

The cutter

The cutter is similar to the sloop, with a single mast rigged both fore and aft. It usually has a mainsail and two headsails. The mast on a cutter is normally set further back than on a sloop. A cutter is sometimes defined by having more than one

Old sailing lore

HALIARDS. Ropes or tackles employed to hoist or lower yards, sails, and flags, upon the masts, yards, stays, &c.

The Elements and Practice of Rigging and Seamanship

headsail. Occasionally a cutter will carry a bowsprit. As it has a greater number of smaller sails than a sloop, the cutter is more easily managed by a small crew and without additional aids.

The ketch

A ketch normally has two masts—a mainmast and a shorter mizzen-mast. The masts are traditionally rigged fore and aft. Jibs are sometimes used as well. The ketch can also carry a spinnaker when sailing before the wind. The layout of the ketch makes it more adaptable than a sloop, especially when sailing in strong winds, as the mainsail can be lowered, leaving the smaller sails to provide necessary propulsion.

Schooner

This is a sailing ship with fore and aft sails on at least two and sometimes more masts. The schooner can carry topsails or jib sails or triangular Bermuda sails. On a schooner, unlike a ketch, the mainmast is the rear mast, and the other mast is the foremast.

Getting a sloop ready for sailing

Fasten the tack of the jib to the bow fitting and hook the luff of the fore-sail to the forestay. Attach the sheets and halyards and hoist the mainsail and make sure it is tensioned correctly. The jib sail is set by attaching the tack to the bow fitting and hanking the sail onto the forestay. Use a bowline to attach the sheets to the clew. Then attach the halyard to the head of the sail. Pass the sheets through the fairleads and on to the cockpit. Tie a stopper knot in the end of each sheet to stop them running back through the fairleads. Once the jib sail has been hoisted to the top, wrap the sheet and the halyard round the appropriate cleat.

Hoisting the spinnaker

The spinnaker can be an unruly sail if not handled carefully. The ropes that control the spinnaker include the foreguy, the spinnaker sheet and the spinnaker guy. To begin with, it can be helpful to clip two sets of sheets and guys together and make sure

the halyard is accessible. Then attach the shackles to the three corners of the sail while it is still in the bag. The spinnaker pole should then be raised and secured. The guy is then connected to the pole and the pole itself is raised using the uphaul. Next secure it with the downhaul. It should be action stations in the cockpit, with someone holding the sheet and someone else holding the guy. The halyard should be hauled from near the mast and the spinnaker raised quickly. The genoa is then lowered.

Mooring

Attach the bow and stern lines to a cleats at the bow and stern, ensuring they are outside the lifelines. Make a loose coil so that they are readily available when necessary. Check that there are fenders deployed on the side of the boat that will touch the mooring and that they are securely fastened. Once alongside, crew can go ashore with the bow and stern lines. Secure the bow and stern lines to the moorings. When the boat leaves, ensure that the bow and stern lines are neatly coiled and stowed away.

There is a variety of mooring lines on a boat, including the stern line, aft breast, fore-spring, aft spring, fore-breast line and bow line. The bow and stern lines should be twice the length of the boat; the springs should be about one-and-a-half times the length of the boat and the breast lines can be the same length of the boat.

Three-stranded nylon lines are probably ideal as mooring lines, as they provide a reasonable amount of stretch to allow for the movement of the boat. Take extra care to protect the lines from wear where they rub against the dockside. Protect the lines at vulnerable points, but check the lines regularly and replace if necessary.

Jury rig

A mast may break and fall overboard. This can happen because a vital part of the rigging, such as the backstay, breaks. The best way to prevent this happening is to inspect the rigging regularly and renew it if necessary. Always take spare halyards on the boat in case anything needs to be replaced.

If the mast does break, it should be hauled in and strapped to the toe rail. You may then have to construct a jury rig to get you home. If the lower part of the mast is still in one piece, you can lash the broken top of the mast back on to the lower part. Then lash the top part of the mainsail to the adapted mast.

The alternative is to create a sprit rig, when the broken piece of mast goes out at a diagonal from half-way up the remaining part of the mainmast. Here the bottom part of the sail is used.

Jury rig

A jury rig is designed to provide sailing power after a boat has been dismasted. The rig is under a temporary arrangement put together from the remains of the broken mast and the yards.

Getting a boat underway

The lines, sheets and halyards are the only means of controlling often unruly sails and spinnakers in unpredictable weather conditions. It is essential, therefore, that you know what all the sheets are for, that they are clean and well maintained and not likely to break under strain. It is important to carry out regular inspections of all of the standing rigging as well as of the shackles and pins that connect them to the boat. Often it is failures in these areas that can lead to a dismasting. The problem may not be down wear; it could be something as straightforward as a missing pin. It is easier to replace one small pin than one large mast. Also check that ropes and lines are clear of any obstructions and have not become wrapped around each other, and that there are no loops lying around that someone is likely to step into and find the line wrapped round their leg.

Before you start setting sail, all ropes and lines should be running free, i.e. not engaged in winches or cleats or tied to anything.

The main-sail halyard is then hauled until the sail reaches its top. Once it is raised, tie off the halyard. The boom can sometimes be secured by a rope extending from its base, which should be tied to a cleat.

The next halyard to be identified is the one for the front sail. Again, this should be hauled until the sail is fully hoisted and tied off to a cleat. The main sheet is then pulled to adjust the main sail on the optimum angle while the jib is being trimmed. For more detail on precise sailing directions, consult the relevant manual.

Of the two jib sheets, pull first on the one on the leeward side. This should trim the jib to stop it flapping in the wind. Then work on the main sail by letting out the main sheet as much as necessary. If either sail starts flapping or luffing, you can either adjust them with the sheets or alter course. To tack when sailing into the wind, turn the boat across the wind, pull the jib sheet out of its cleat and wait for the main sail and boom to cross over to the other side of the boat. Then pull in the jib sheet on the other side on either a cleat or a winch. Once the tack is complete, the sheet should be released from the winch on the windward side and the sheet pulled to leeward.

Dinghy Handling

Often a dinghy is used to go to and from a boat that may be moored in a bay. When coming alongside to unload passengers or supplies, a draw hitch may be a good option as a temporary tether. The advantage of this knot is that it can be undone easily by pulling the end. If the dinghy is to be secured for a longer period and more reliably, it should be tied to the boat with a bowline or secured to a cleat.

Towing a dinghy

When towing a dinghy, it can be tied to the back of the yacht with a chain hitch. The painter can be lengthened if necessary with a carrick bend. The advantage of this knot is that it can take all the strain and jerking on the rope that will occur while the dinghy is being towed, and yet can be untied easily when necessary.

Bringing a dinghy aboard

It is possible to create a system out of knots to haul the dinghy in. Attach the painter first to the bow of the dinghy and then create a bowline in a bight above the centre of the dinghy. Leave a loop that can be engaged with a shackle. Then take the painter either through the stern ring and create a rolling hitch or pass it through the two seat brackets on either side at the back and then create a rolling hitch on the standing part.

Chain hitch

To tie up a dinghy temporarily to a mooring, the chain hitch is a useful knot, being easy to tie and untie and relatively secure.

To tie, create a bight and pass it under the mooring and back over. Then create a second bight and tuck this through the first. Then pass the end under the standing part and pass a small bight through the second bight. Then pull the end under the standing part and tuck another bight through the third bight. The end can be passed through the standing part. At each stage, pull the bight to tighten the knot.

Chain hitch

The chain hitch is a method of attaching a rope to a piece of timber or anything similar that needs to be pulled along. It forms a secure binding and has a locking effect as it is pulled.

Self-tailing winch

A self-tailing winch is a mechanical device with a spool and crank that is used to trim a line on a sailing boat. They often have a stripper or cleat to maintain the tension on the line.

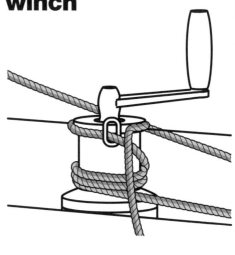

Winches

Sailing a reasonably sized yacht, such as a Bermuda sloop, requires a decent knowledge of how to use winch. Many of these useful devices are designed for one person to use and are known as self-tailers. The winch drum is fitted with a spring-operated track. The winch has a spool and a hand crank as well as a stripper arm and a jam cleat at its top. When a rope is coiled round the winch, the final turn is placed in the track.

To trim a line on a yacht, the crew member turns the handle with one hand and pulls on the loose end with the other to maintain tension. The line is taken around the winch clockwise.

The ratchet on a typical yacht winch allows the handle to be positioned in such a way so that the crew member can get in the best position for optimum leverage.

Winches can be geared to vary the amount of speed and power required for different circumstances. The slow-speed gear means more power.

Occasionally when using a winch you will get an overriding turn which prevents the line from feeding off the drum. An impasse often develops whereby the line can go neither one way nor the other. One solution is to take the end counter-clockwise round the drum and then lead it clockwise around another winch. The force from the other winch is sometimes enough to pull out the trapped bight.

If this does not work, you can bend another line to the standing part of the jammed line with a rolling hitch, then take the new line to another winch to relieve the strain.

Coils
Common coil
This is an easy-to-use coil that keeps the rope available when necessary. The coil is made in the left hand, leaving about 1.2m (4ft) on the end of the rope. Next make a turn counter-clockwise under the coil, around the back to the front. Then take a bight through the coil from front to back, going above the turn at the back. Take the end and pass it through the bight.

Cleat coil
As its name suggests, this is the usual method of securing the halyard end to a cleat in such a way as to prevent tangles and to make it instantly available.

Take the coil in your left hand, leaving about 25cm (10in) of the standing part between the coil and the cleat. Then pass your right hand through the coil, grip the standing part and pull it through the coil. Then hook the bight that has been formed over the top part of the cleat.

Gasket coil
This form of coil is sometimes used when there is no option to hang the

coil on a cleat. It is easy to tie and reliably secure.

Coil the line, leaving about 1.2m (4ft) at the end. Then take three or four turns round the coil with the free end, leaving an eye about 15cm (6in) long. Keep coiling until you have about 0.6m (2ft) of line left.

Then create a 30cm (12in) bight and pass it through the eye of the coil, then pull it back over the top of the coil. Next pull it down against the round turns you have previously made. Then tighten everything up so it is secure.

Stowage coil
This is another secure way of securing and stowing a coil.

Create a coil in the left hand and then create a bight of about 0.6m (2ft) in length. Then take the bight behind the coil and pull it through again. Gudie the bight under the previous bight on the left of the previous tuck. Take this bight behind the coil and pull it through the coil again. Then take the bight from left to right under the standing part of the bight on top of the coil.

Heaving a line
First of all check that you have enough rope to reach the boat or pier you are throwing the line to. You should hold some coils in one hand and throw the rope by swinging your arm back and leaning your opposite shoulder towards the target. Aim well

Common coil

The common coil is an efficient way of storing rope where it is hung in neat coils, tied off and suspended, ready for use.

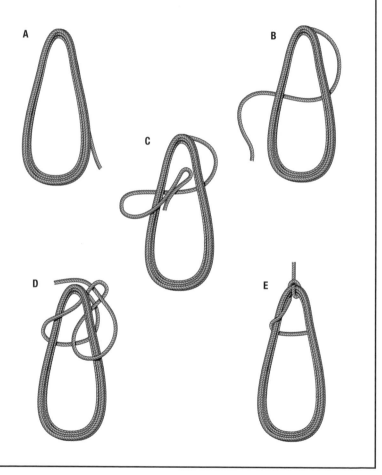

A

B

C

D

E

Cleat coil

The cleat coil is specially adapted to hang from a cleat once a line has been tied off on the cleat. It is designed so that the coil will be free of knots or tangles when it is laid on the deck.

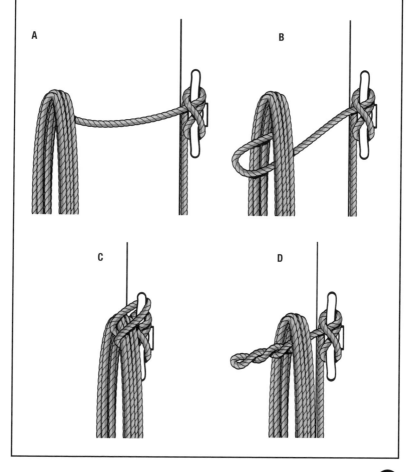

A

B

C

D

Gasket coil

This is an alternative way of coiling a rope where it may not be possible to hang the rope off a solid object such as a cleat. It is also a secure way of storing a rope.

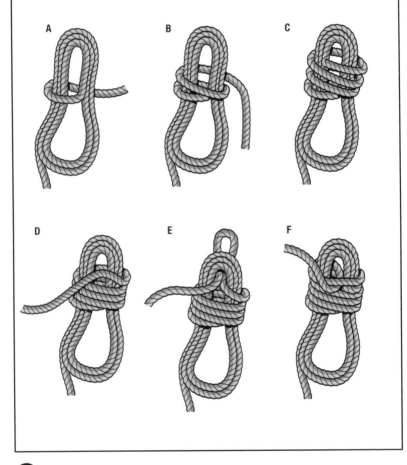

A

B

C

D

E

F

Stowage coil

The stowage coil allows the rope to be neatly coiled while also providing a useful loop from which it can be hung.

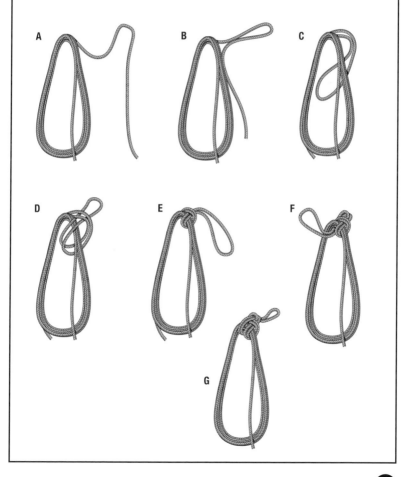

above the target. If the rope misses the target, bring it in quickly to avoid it getting fouled on the propeller.

Maritime Knots
Sheepshank
This knot is sometimes used for temporarily shortening a line. First create an s-shape with the rope and make a half hitch above the right-hand loop. Then do

the same for the left-hand loop. Once you have pulled tight, there will be two small loops held by the half hitches. The next step is to bind the two loops to the standing parts so that the sheepshank does not fall apart.

Jury knot
This knot is designed specifically for the process of setting up a jury

Heaving a line

In order to heave or throw a line successfully it is important to ensure that the rope is properly coiled and that it will not tangle or snag when it is thrown. It may not be possible to throw all the rope coils at one time.

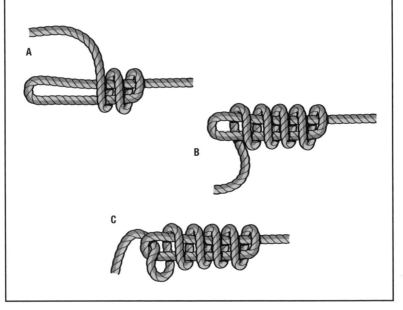

Sheepshank

The sheepshank is a useful method of shortening
a piece of rope, but take care that the knot does not fall
apart when it is not under strain. It can be useful for
bypassing a frayed part of a rope.

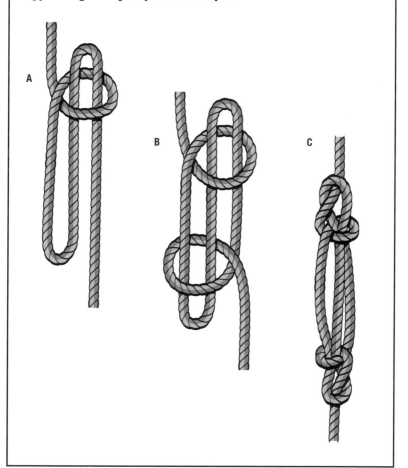

A

B

C

Jury knot

The jury knot is associated with the jury rig. There is an area at the centre for the mast itself and the various loops are designed to hold stays and shrouds.

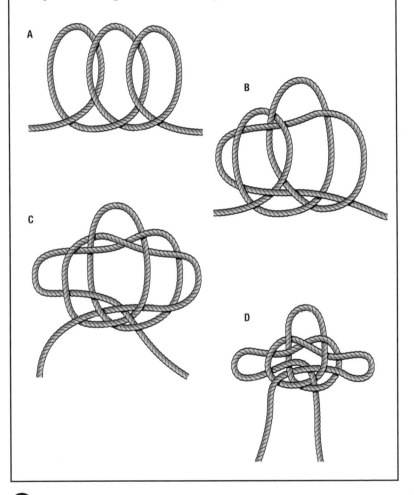

rig after dismasting. It consists of a main loop, which goes over what remains of the mast, and some secondary loops which are designed to hold any stays or shrouds to the mast.

To begin, make three overhand loops. The size of the first loop should depend on the diameter of the mast. The second loop should be larger. Move the left edge of the second overhand loop under the right edge of the first overhand loop. The left edge of the third overhand loop should be placed under the right edge of the second overhand loop. Then weave the overhand loops together by placing the left edge of the right overhand loop on the top of the right edge of the left overhand loop. Continue the process by placing the right edge of the left overhand loop over the right edge of the centre overhand loop and by placing the left edge of the right overhand under the left edge of the centre overhand loop. Finish by placing the right edge of the left overhand loop under the right edge of the left overhand loop under the right edge of the right overhand loop and by placing the left edge of the right overhand loop over the left edge of the left overhand loop. Once the knot is complete, place it over the mast and pull tight. Attach guy lines to the loops with Becket hitches.

Gaff topsail halyard bend

The name of this knot is certainly redolent of the sea. It is a secure knot and has the advantage of being compact.

To begin, pass the line under the post or spar that you are tying-on to. Then take it round again, bringing the working end round to the standing part. Then take the working end behind the standing part and slip it along the spar under the two loops you had made. Then pull tight.

Ossel knot

This knot is used to tie a line or rope to a post or spar. It has connections with the sea and fishing, as the word 'ossel' is the Scottish word for a gill net.

To begin, take a turn round either a rope or a spar by passing the line in front of the object and over the back and round again. Cross the line diagonally over the standing part and then take another turn round the object. Then bring the working end round again and take it round for a second turn. Next take a turn round to the right of the standing part. Pull up a bight from the standing part by pulling it off the top of the object and pass the working end through the bight. Then pull on the standing part to trap the working end.

Boom hitch

This knot is both easy to tie and relatively secure.

To start, place the working end over the spar or pole from front to back at

Gaff topsail halyard bend

A halyard is a line that is used to pull up a yard or sail. This knot was designed to be secure, as well as relatively flat, to minimize the gap between the spar and the sail.

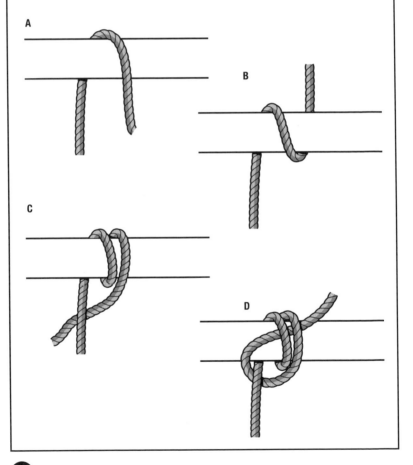

A

B

C

D

a diagonal. Bring the end round and across its own standing part. Then take it round the spar again at the opposite diagonal. Bring it round again and cross it over at the same angle as the first turn. Then bring it round again to the front, to the right of the standing part. Take it from right to left over the standing part again and then round to the front once more. Now pass the working end over the left-most turn and under the next one in. At this point pull everything tight.

Cat's paw

This ingenious knot allows you to spread the load between two separate loops, which provides extra security. The general idea is that if one loop should break the other is there to hold the load.

First form a bight either from a strop or by doubling a line. Then bend the bight over to form two loops, turned in opposite directions. Then twist each loop so that they are strengthened by the turn. Continue turning the loops up to about four twists each. Then place both loops over the hook or whatever anchor is being used. Pull on both standing parts together to tighten the arrangement.

Anchor bend

This knot is used for tying a line or rope to either a ring or some other attachment. As its name suggests,

the ring is often part of an anchor. The anchor bend is usually quite easy to untie, though it is sometimes prone to jamming. An extra turn round the ring or other object makes jamming less likely.

To begin, pass the working end over and round the attachment point. Then take it round again to the front. Take it round in front of the standing part and pass it through the two round turns you had previously made. Then tie two half hitches, leaving a reasonable length of working end to avoid slippage or the knot becoming untied.

Halter hitch

This knot has traditionally been used for tethering animals such as horses and it provides reasonable security while also being easy to undo. The only problem is that it can sometimes be undone, either inadvertently or intentionally, by animal.

If feeding through a ring, take the working end through the back of the ring then cross it over its own standing part. Take it behind the standing part and form a bight in the working end. Then tuck in the bight to form a running overhand knot and a loop before finally passing the working end through the drawloop.

Mooring hitch

This knot is ideal for mooring small boats where the tide may be rising and

Ossel knot

The word 'ossel' is the Scottish word for a gill net.
This knot is used to tie a line/rope to a post or spar.

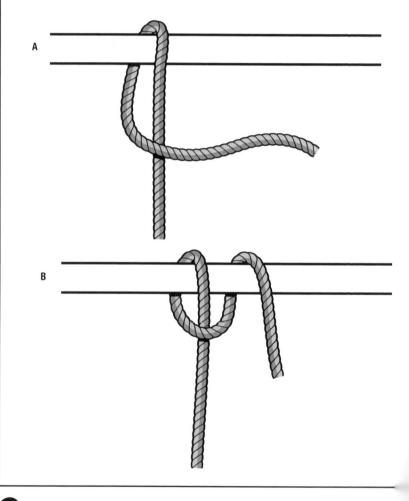

A

B

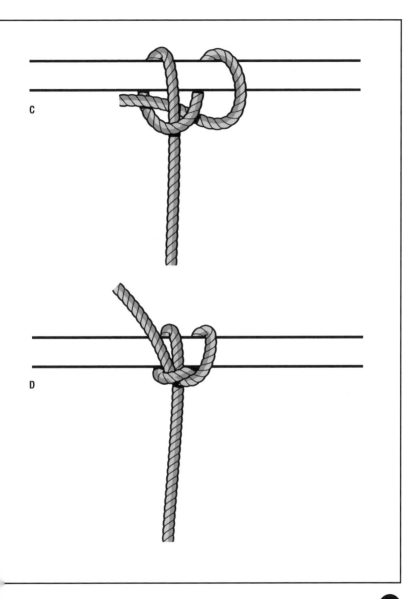

C

D

Boom hitch

The boom hitch is a secure knot that is used to attach a rope or line to the boom of a sail or to any other fixed object.

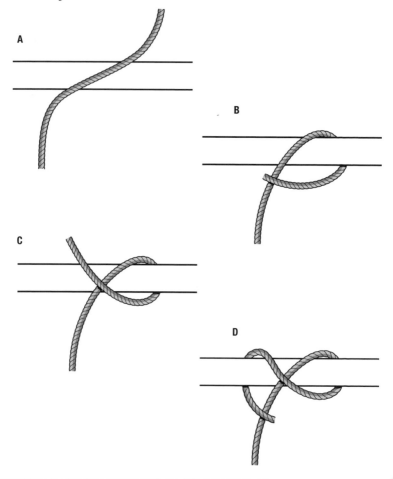

A

B

C

D

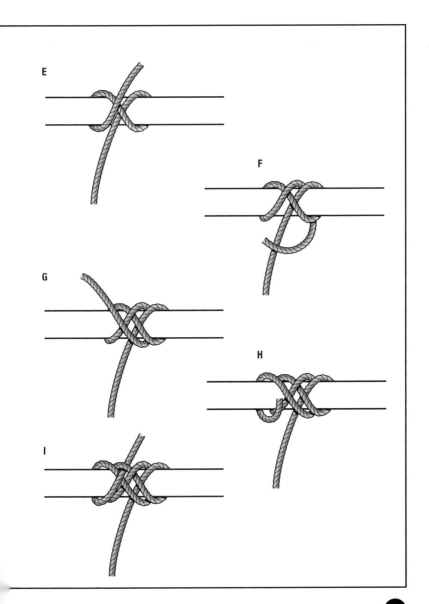

E

F

G

H

I

Cat's paw

The Cat's paw knot is similar to the cow hitch, and is a method of attaching a rope to an object such as a ring or a hook.

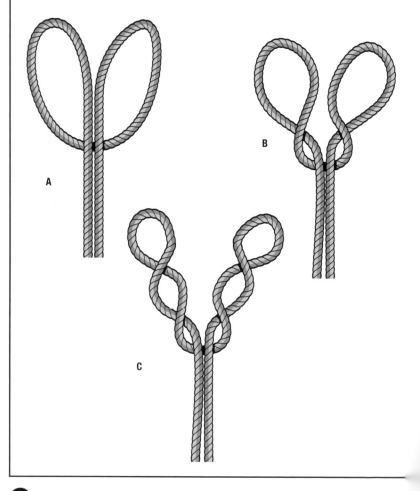

A

B

C

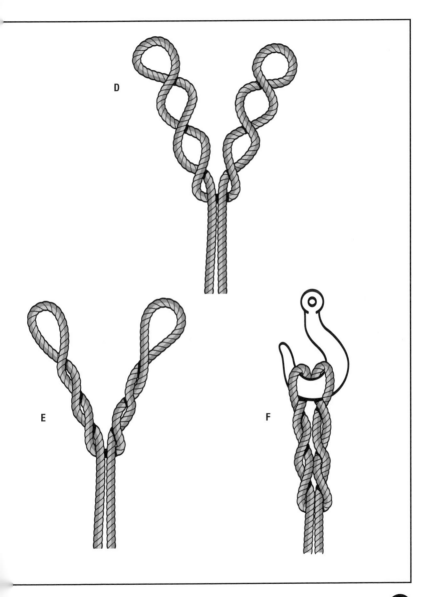

D

E

F

183

falling, as the knot can be easily adjusted. It can also be quickly released.

Take the working end round the mooring attachment from back to front. Then make an underhand loop and place it over the standing part. Then make a bight in the working end and pass it under the standing part and over the top of the end of the loop. Then pull everything tight to finish.

Sheets

Sheets are ropes that are normally attached to the corner of a sail, and they control the angle of the sail to the wind. The unusual name is derived from Old English *sceata*, meaning corner of the sail.

The sheets on a typical modern rig, such as a Bermuda rig, are normally divided into three main categories— the main sheet, the jib sheet and the spinnaker sheet. The main sheet is

Old sailing lore

SHEET, (écoute, Fr.) a rope fastened to one or both the lower corners of a sail, to extend and retain it in a particular station. See CLUE and SAIL.

When a ship sails with a lateral wind, the lower corner of the main and fore sail are fastened by a tack and a sheet; the former being to windward and the latter to leeward: the tack, however, is entirely difused with a stern wind; whereas the sail is never spread without the assistance of one or both of the sheets.

The stay-sails and studding-sails have only one tack and one sheet each: the stay-sail tacks are always fastened forward, and the sheet drawn aft; but the studding-sail-tack draws the outer clue of the sail to the extremity of the bottom; whereas the sheet is employed to extend the inmost.

William Falconer's *Dictionary of the Marine*

Halter hitch

The halter hitch would typically be used to tether a horse to a ring or pole, but it can be used in other contexts as well. The advantage of this hitch is that it can be quickly released.

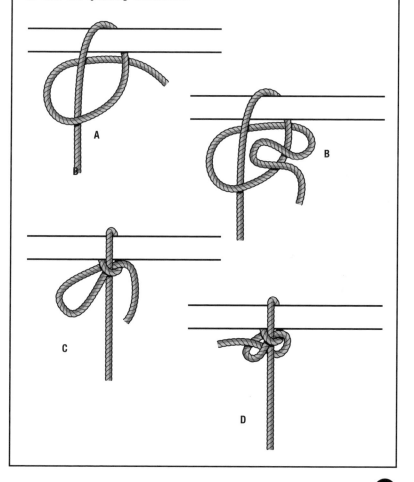

Mooring hitch

The mooring hitch is similar to the halter hitch, to the extent that it can be used to tether a boat or an animal while being easy to undo when quick-release is required.

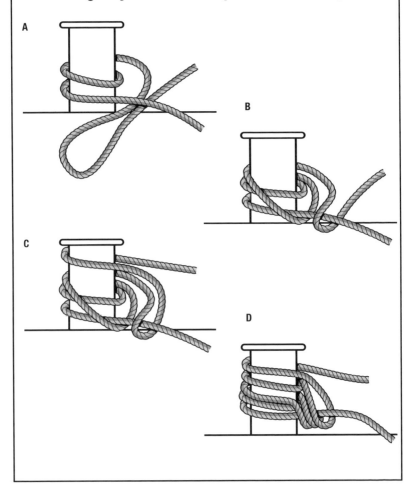

the sheet that controls the main sail and is normally attached to the boom. If there is no boom, it is attached to the main sail clew.

The jib sheets are attached to the clew of the jib (fore-sail) and control it on one side or another. The jib sheets run down either side of the boat and only one of them is operative at any time.

The spinnaker sheets are attached to the clews on both the bottom corners of the spinnaker. They are sometimes run through blocks to winches adjacent to the cockpit of the boat. The spinnaker sheets are sometimes backed up by spinnaker guys.

Control Lines
Guys
The guys are used to control the spars on a sailing boat, which normally means the spinnaker pole on a Bermuda rig.

The guy attached to the spinnaker that runs through the end of the spinnaker pole is known as the working guy, among other terms. The guy pulls the pole round the mast, depending on the direction of the wind, and it is controlled from near the cockpit. When the boat jibes and the spinnaker pole moves from one side to the other, what was previously the guy becomes the sheet.

A foreguy or spinnaker pole downhaul controls the height of the spinnaker pole and stops it lifting up in strong winds. It can also be used

to provide some measure on control on the sail.

Types of Sailing Knot and Rope Care
As with mountain climbing, there is some division in sailing between ropes that have a certain amount of stretch and those that don't. For sheets, a polyester or double-braid rope can be used. For halyards, where wire is not used, a strong Kevlar, Dyneema or Spectra rope might be suitable. Another advantage of these advanced materials is that they have a light weight but high strength, and they can save a lot of weight, which is useful when racing.

Simple hitch/half hitch
This is unreliable as a holding knot on its own, but it can be doubled to form two half hitches or it can be used to finish off other, stronger knots. Put the working end through an object such as a ring, holding the standing part in the left hand. Pull the working end through and then over the standing part. Then pull the working end through the bight that has been created. Then tighten the knot. When pulling the working end through the bight you can make a bight out of the working end and pull this through.

Stevedore's knot
This is a stopper knot that can be used as an alternative to other

Old sailing lore

DOWNHAULER. A rope which hoists down the stay-sails, studding sails, and boom-sails, to shorten sail, &c.

The Elements and Practice of Rigging and Seamanship

stopper knots, such as the figure of eight.

To begin, make a loop out of a twisted bight at one end. Then twist the loop again, then again with a half twist, followed by another half twist.

Then take the working end and pass it through the loop and pull the knot tight, with the working end forced against the main part of the knot.

Cunningham knot

A Cunningham is a variation on the downhaul and was invented by an Americas' Cup captain of that name to optimize both speed and control.

Here a line is secured at one end of the boom and passed through a cringle on the sail then down to the securing point, either on the deck or the mast or the boom itself. The Cunningham provides fine adjustment of the tension of the luff.

Becket hitch

The name for this hitch derived from the eye loop, or 'becket', which it is tied onto. It is in effect the same knot as a sheet bend.

Take the working end through the loop from the back, then pass it round behind the neck of the loop, bringing it round to the front again where it is passed under its own standing part and in front of the bottom right side of the loop.

Carrick bend

This knot is both decorative and useful, and also seems to have a long history. It was probably used by merchant seamen and fighting navies. It joins two lines together.

To start the Carrick bend, make a loop with one of the working ends. Bring the second line over the working end and then take it under the standing part of the first line. Start another loop and tuck the second working end under the first loop, over its own standing part and then under the first loop again. Pull on the two standing parts to tighten the knot so it is secure.

Older forms of the knot were prevented from capsizing by binding the two working ends to the standing part. This would have retained its decorative symmetrical look.

Simple hitch/half hitch

Simple hitch/half hitch. This knot is a form of overhand knot where the working end is brought over and then under the standing part. Although it is not a very secure knot on its own, it is often used as an addition to other knots.

A

B

Stevedore's knot

The Stevedore's knot is a form of stopper knot that is bulkier than the standard figure-of-eight knot, but which is less likely to jam. It has one more wrap round the standing part than a figure-of-eight.

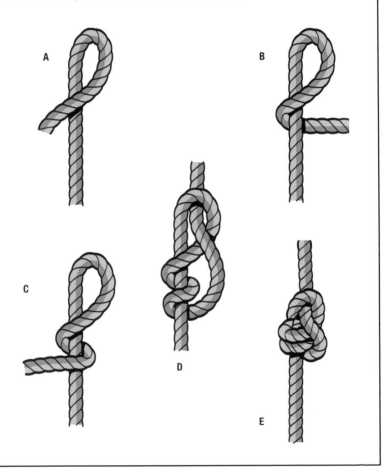

A

B

C

D

E

Becket hitch

The becket hitch is designed to tie a rope to the becket, or eye, of a pulley or any other form of loop or handle. Otherwise, it is similar to a sheet bend.

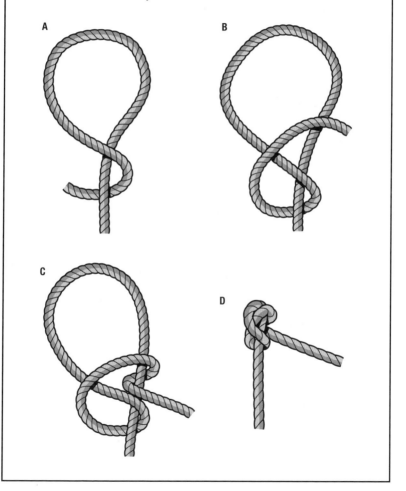

A

B

C

D

Carrick bend

The Carrick bend is often used for joining heavy rope or any form of line that is difficult to manipulate. It has the advantage of being relatively easy to untie even when it has been under strain.

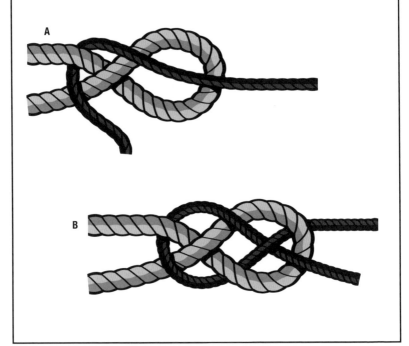

Lighterman's hitch/towboat hitch

This hitch is often used for towing or mooring large vessels and can stand a great deal of strain. Its ingenious design, however, means that the lighterman's hitch also never fully tightens, so it can be thrown off with relative ease after it has been under strain. To tie, pass the working end round the object (such as a mooring or tow bar). Make a complete turn round the object. Keep a fairly long working end free, as various things need to be done with it. Make a bight from the working end and take it under the standing part and over the object. Then bring the working end over the standing part, taking round the object.

Constrictor knot

This knot has a number of uses, such as seizing the ends of ropes.

It is similar to the clove hitch in its early stages and is ideally used with a relatively narrow line.

Take the cord, rope or line round whatever is to be tied on to and then bring the working end back and over across its own standing part. Take the working end over the object again and then bring it back to be passed under the diagonal made earlier. Then pass the working end under the first turn and pull it through. At this point, tighten the knot by pulling on the working end and the standing part.

Draw hitch

This hitch is sometimes known as the highwayman's hitch, which covers its usefulness both for tethering a horse or tying up a boat temporarily. It is therefore a serviceable knot for everyday use, but not one that can be relied on in extreme circumstances or under extreme strain. It can be quickly untied by pulling on the free working end.

The knot is made up essentially of three open bights. Start by doubling the end of the rope to form the first bight and then pass it under and behind the object. Then take the standing part of the rope and form a second bight and push that from in front and over the top of the object through the first bight. Tighten the knot so it holds in place at this stage then take the working end and form a third bight. Push this through the second bight from front to back. You can now pull on the standing part to test the knot.

Trucker's hitch

This hitch is also sometimes known as the waggoner's hitch or dolly. For sailing purposes, it can be used temporarily to secure a halyard or it can be used for a number of other purposes, such as tying down a dinghy or raft.

It is best to ensure that one end of the rope is fixed before starting this knot. Create a small loop by lifting up the hanging free end of line. Then create a bight. Form a crossing turn further up the standing part and pass the bight through that from back to front. Now pull on the newly formed loop and make two twists. Then pull the free end of the rope through the loop with the twists to make another loop, which should then be put round a hook or other retainer. To tighten the knot, pull on the free end of rope.

To make fast to a cleat is an

Lighterman's hitch / towboat hitch

The lighterman's hitch is designed for towing where considerable loads are involved. The beauty of the knot is that it can be easily released even when it has been subjected to great strain, and it will not jam.

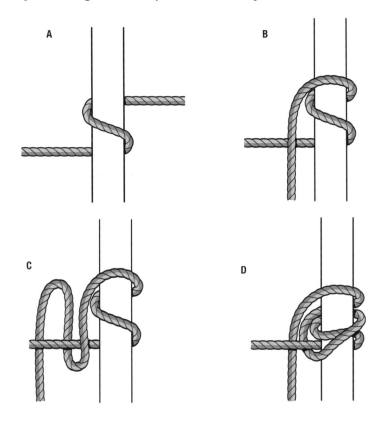

A

B

C

D

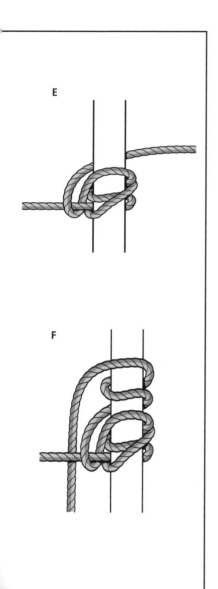

E

F

important exercise for anyone who uses a boat, as when mooring a boat the vessel needs to be tied quickly and efficiently. It it also needs to be cast off without danger of jamming in order to avoid possible damage to the boat. Take the line round the side of the cleat at an angle away from the line and take it round to the other side of the cleat. Make one turn. Then cross over the centre of the cleat with a figure-of-eight turn. Then tie a single hitch.

Short splice

This splice is designed for two pieces of rope of the same kind and the same diameter. The result is a strong join in the rope, but the diameter of the rope around the splice will increase, which may cause the rope to jam if it is run through a block or a ring that has little extra room.

The two lengths of rope should be unlaid (unravelled) up to about 10cm (4in). Each unlaid strand of one rope should be placed between the unlaid strands of the other rope. Then grasp the unlaid strands of both ropes and pull them so that they become firmly intertwined. Then take one unlaid strand and pass it over the nearest strand of the opposite rope and under the next strand. Carry out the same process with the other strands, one by one. Then pull the rope strands in the opposite direction and repeat the process of tucking strands over the one next to it and under the next

Constrictor knot

The constrictor knot is an effective binding knot which, although it is intended to be quick release fixing, can be difficult to undo once it is tightened.

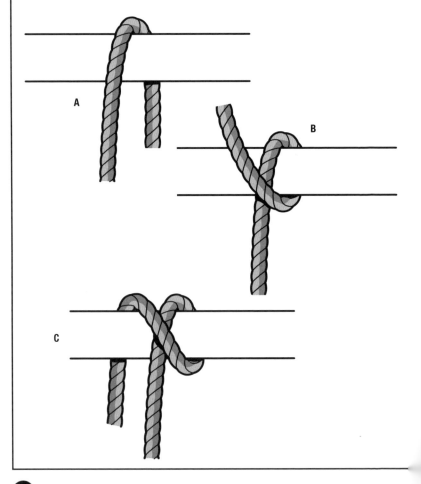

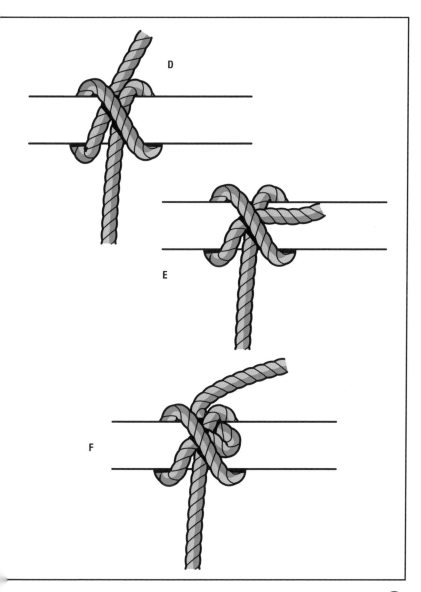

D

E

F

Old sailing lore

CLEATS. Pieces of wood of various shapes, used for stops, and to make ropes fast to, viz. ARM or SLING-CLEATS are nailed on each side of the slings of the lower yard, and have an arm at one end, which lies over the straps of the jeer blocks to prevent their being chaffed. BELAYING-CLEATS have two arms, or horns, and are nailed through the middle to the masts, or elsewhere, to belay ropes to. COMB-CLEATS are semi-circular, and are hollowed in the middle to confine a rope to one place. RANGE-CLEATS are shaped like belaying-cleats, but are much larger, and are bolted through the middle. SHROUD-CLEATS have two arms, similar to belaying-cleats; the inside is hollowed to fit the shroud, and grooves are cut round the middle and ends to receive the seizings, which confine them to the shrouds. STOP-CLEATS are nailed to yard-arms, to prevent the slipping of the rigging and the gammoning, and to stop collars on masts, &c. THUMB-CLEATS are shaped like arm-cleats, but are much smaller.

The Elements and Practice of Rigging and Seamanship

Old sailing lore

To BELAY, (amarrer, Fr. from beleygen, Beig.) to fasten a rope by winding it several times round a cleat, belaying-pin, or kevel: this term is peculiar to small ropes, and chiefly the running-rigging, there being several other expressions used for large ropes, as bitting, bending, making fast, stopping, &c.

William Falconer's *Dictionary of the Marine*

Trucker's hitch

The trucker's hitch is a useful hitch for securing loads, and it has been used for many years on horse-drawn waggons as well as on modern transport. It has an effect similar to a block and tackle.

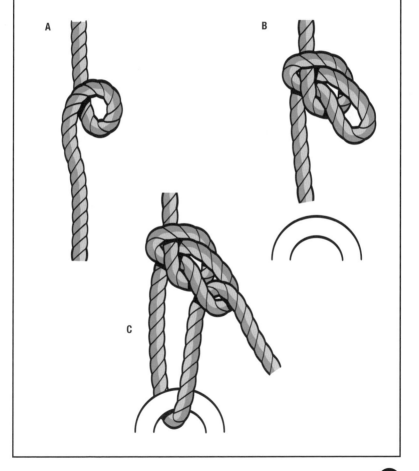

A

B

C

Eye splice

The eye splice is a means of creating a permanent loop at the end of a multi-stranded rope. The strands of the rope are plaited back.

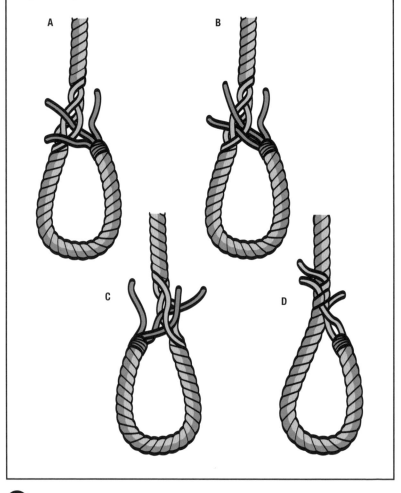

Short splice

The short splice maintains a great deal of strength in the rope, but it also increases the diameter of the rope to a greater proportion than the other splices do.

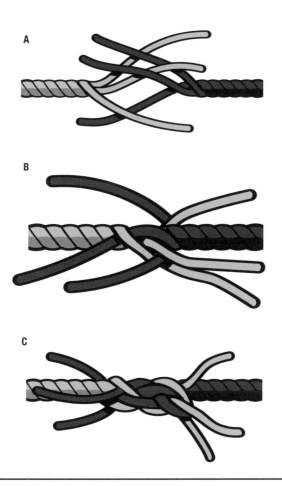

A

B

C

Long splice

The long splice creates a much smoother finish to the joined rope and one where the diameter is not much greater than the original rope. However, it is not as strong as the thicker short splice.

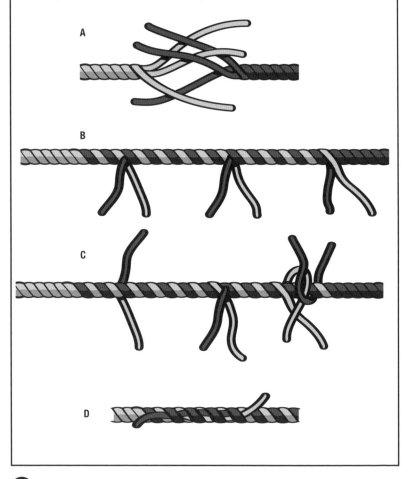

strand. Then do the same for the other two strands. The strands can then be either trimmed or tapered.

Long splice

This splice is designed for occasions where you need the rope to run smoothly, for example through a block or a narrow ring. The downside of this splice is that it is not as strong as the short splice.

First unlay a reasonable amount of both ropes and then place each strand between the unlaid strands of the opposite rope, as with the short splice. Do the same as with the short splice, which is to pull the unlaid strands firmly together. Then unlay a strand in one rope for a few twists and twist round in its place an unlaid strand from the other rope. Continue this process (unlaying one strand and replacing it with another) until you have almost run out of length of the replacement strand. Then repeat this process with other strands— unbinding one and replacing with another. Once this process is complete, tie overhand knots with the strand ends. Once you have tied the overhand knots, take each strand end and pass it over the second strand of the overhand knot. Then tuck it under the first laid strand and then over and under the next two laid strands. Then do the same for the other strand ends of the overhand knots. The ends should then be trimmed.

Backsplice

This useful splice is designed to prevent the end of a rope from fraying and unlaying.

To begin, put a temporary whipping or a piece of tape round the point where you plan to start the splice. Then unlay the rope until you reach the stop and tie a crown knot (see p.207) with the unlaid ends.

The unlaid ends will now be layered into the standing end of rope below the crown knot. Take the strand and pass it over the first laid strand below the crown knot and under the second laid strand. Then continue the process further down the standing part for the second and third strands. Do the same for the other unlaid ends.

Heaving line bend

This knot is used to attach a light line to a thicker piece of rope or heavy hawser so it can be pulled within reach.

To begin, create a bight in the heavier rope and lay the light line down over the bight. Then take the working end of the line round and over the standing part of the thick rope bight, under and back again over its own standing part. Then pass the working end under the short strand of the rope bight and bring it back round and across the bight to tuck under the loop that was created in the line on the left-hand side of the bight.

Backsplice

The backsplice, which is also known as an end splice, is the traditional method of finishing the end of a rope so as to prevent fraying. It creates a significant increase in thickness.

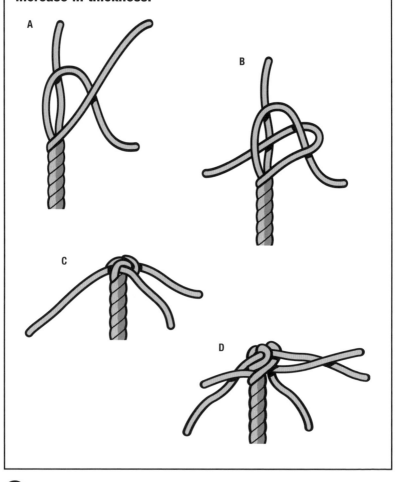

Heaving line bend

The purpose of the heaving line bend is to attach a line to a heavy hawser so that it can be drawn into place. It goes without saying that the bend needs to be extremely secure.

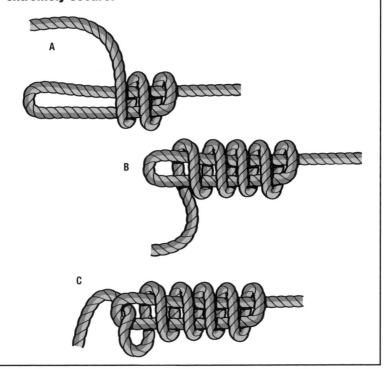

Monkey's fist

This knot was designed to increase the weight and mass on the end of a line so it can be thrown with greater accuracy and a greater chance of reaching its target. Although the weight on the line will be increased by the mass of the knot alone, it is also possible to incorporate a weight within the knot to give it extra weight. If a weight is incorporated, make sure that it is not thrown directly at a

Monkey's fist

The monkey's fist has traditionally been tied in a line as a weight when throwing a heaving line, but it can also be used as a weapon and as a decoration. It can be tied round a weight for added effect.

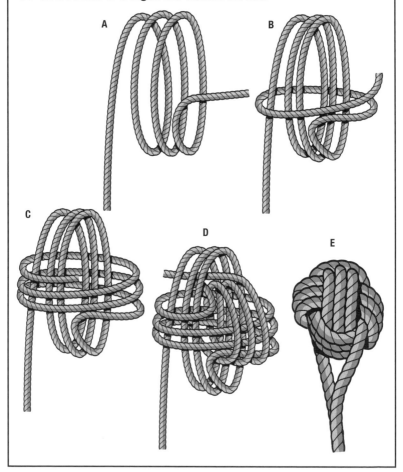

person who may be receiving the line. In fact, the monkey's fist has in the past been used as a weapon. An alternative to a weight is to insert floating material such as cork within the monkey's fist which will keep it afloat if it is being thrown over water. To begin, take the line three times round your hand so that the turns are side-by-side. Then make three turns round the first three, horizontally. Then pass the working end through the top of the knot between the two sets of turns. Do the same at the bottom of the knot between the two sets of turns. Then make three more turns to create a globe. Before tightening, you can insert a weight or float as appropriate or leave it empty. The turns should be tightened consecutively and with care so that the knot maintains its even shape.

Wall knot

This is a useful knot, similar to the crown knot, and which is sometimes used as the basis for other knots.

Start by unlaying the strands of a rope, leaving plenty of length to work with. Pass one strand under the second strand anti-clockwise. The third strand end is then taken round and under the first strand end and then under the third strand end. Then take the third strand end and pass it through a bight in the first strand. At this point you can tighten all the strands to finish the knot.

Wall knot

This knot can be used on its own or as the basis of a variety of other knots. It is similar to the crown knot.

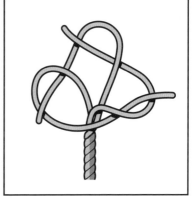

Crown knot

This knot is used as a base for some other knots and is made in three-stranded rope.

The ends of the rope are first unlaid, leaving sufficient length of ends to work with. The first strand is laid over the second strand end, leaving a bight. The second strand is then passed over the first strand and then over the third. The third strand is then taken over the second strand and then passed through the bight created at the beginning of the process. Then carefully tighten the various strands.

Crown knot

The crown knot can be tied in a three-stranded rope in order to prevent fraying or to create a decorative end.

A

B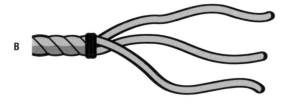

C

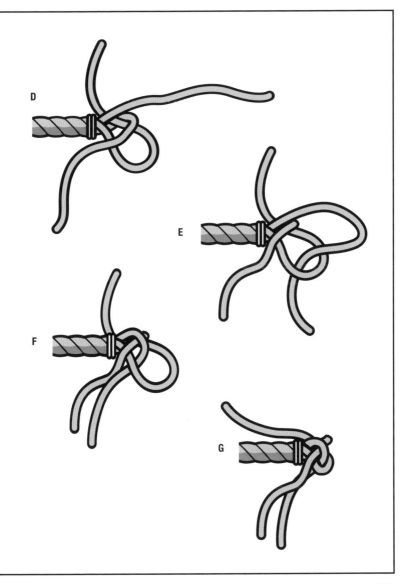

D

E

F

G

Double grinner knot

This knot can be used to tie together two sections of fishing line. First lay the lines side by side and tie one grinner knot, which entails taking one line back to form a bight, then passing over the other line and round to catch the standing part of the bight, repeating the process about three times. Then tighten the first grinner knot. Now repeat the process, using the second line to tie-on to the first line to form the second grinner knot. Then pull the knots together to form the double grinner.

Ashley's bend

This is a handy knot as it is both secure and relatively easy to untie once it has been put under strain.

First make a crossing turn with the first rope, placing the working end under the standing part. Then take the second line and pass it through the loop that has been made in the first line and then under its own standing part in the same way. Now take both working ends through the two turns that have been created. The knot can be tightened at this point by pulling on the working ends and the standing part. Then take the ends of each standing part and finish the tightening process.

Hunter's bend

Sometimes known as the rigger's bend, this knot is practical for being both secure and easy to untie once it

has been under strain. It can also be tied in a variety of rope materials.

The hunter's bend consists of two overhand knots that are linked together. Place the lines to be joined side by side from opposite directions. Then take one working end round the back and pass it through the loops. Take the other working end and do the same thing from front to back (i.e. in reverse). At this point, begin to tighten up the knot, pulling on each working end and standing part.

Racking bend

This knot is used for attaching a light line to something like a heavy hawser or rope. The knot is designed to be secure, providing a firm hold on the bight of the hawser. It also keeps the two sides of the bight in the hawser together.

First make a bight in the larger rope or hawser and pass the thinner line over the end of the bight. Then take the working end of the line under one side of the bight then back over and across the bight, passing it under the other side of the bight. Then bring it round, over and across the bight again, taking it under the other side of the bight. This process can be continued for as many turns as will make the hold on the bight and the rope or hawser completely secure.

To finish the knot, pass the working end under the last racking turn and then work down the various parts of

Double grinner knot

The double grinner knot is often used in fishing circles to join two monofilament lines. It does not matter if the two lines are of different diameters. The two sides of the knot are tightened independently.

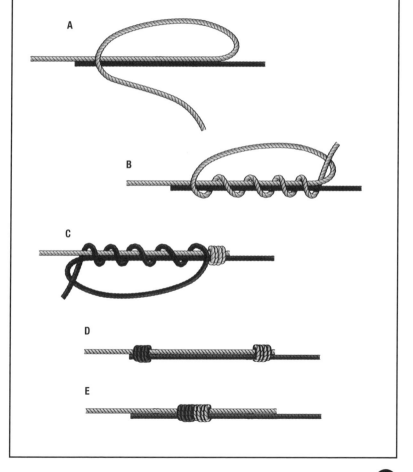

A

B

C

D

E

Ashley's bend

The Ashley's bend knot is formed from two interlocking overhand knots and it is very secure. It can withstand considerable strain as well as movement. It is often used to tie two lines together to make a longer line.

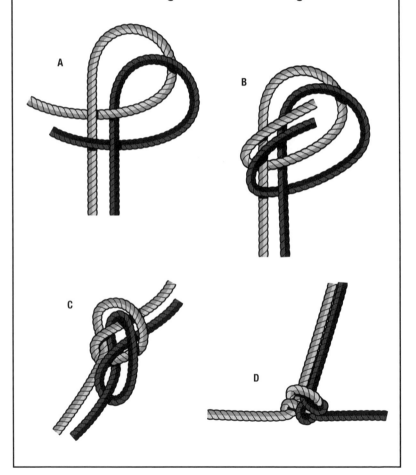

A

B

C

D

Hunter's bend

The Hunter's bend is sometimes known as a rigger's bend, and consists of a two interlocking overhand knots. It is a relatively recent knot, which has been 'invented' independently on two separate occasions.

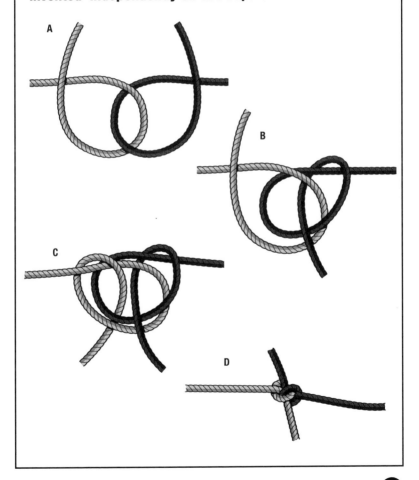

the knot, tightening each strand rather as you would tighten shoe laces.

Zeppelin bend

This knot is known to have been used to moor airships. It is a secure knot that works best with two ropes of roughly equal diameter.

Take two ropes and hold them together in the same direction. Then form a loop with one rope. Take the working end of the rope in which you have just formed the loop behind both ropes and back through the loop. Then grasp the standing part of the other rope and move it upwards towards the top of the loop. Take the working end of the second rope under its standing part and through the loop. Then pull on both working ends and standing parts to tighten the knot and make it secure.

Adjustable bend

This knot, which was invented by a climber, can be used for tying guy ropes. Generally the knots are tied separately, and remain separate. If put under a sharp strain, the knots may come together and, in doing so, provide some shock absorption.

To start, place the two ropes side by side from opposite ends. Take one line round the other and then repeat. Then take the working end round the other line and its own standing part. Then take the working end over the other rope and pass it under the last turn.

Now take the other line and repeat the process, tying it onto the first line.

Whipping and Seizing

There are a variety of techniques for whipping (see the box opposite for an explanation of this term). Although whipping techniques are centuries old, they are as relevant today as they always have been. The advantage of whipping over heat-sealing is that it is more reliable, as heat-sealing tends to break down over time.

Common whipping

This technique can be used for three-stranded and braided rope. Use natural twine for natural ropes and synthetic twine for synthetic ropes.

Make a bight with the twine and lay it along the length of the rope. Wrap the twine first underneath and then round the rope so that the twine loop is trapped. Leave a short tail at the back of the loop before wrapping. Keep on with the wrapping action, heading towards the end of the rope. Make sure these wraps are made in the opposite direction to the lay of the rope. Continue with the whipping until it is as long as the diameter of the rope or a bit longer.

Then pass the working end of twine through the remaining part of the original bight. Next pull the bight under the turns by pulling on the short tail you left when you started making the turns round the rope. Then trim the ends of the twine.

Racking bend

The racking bend knot is used to join two ropes of different diameters. The racking effect is the weaving of the smaller diameter rope round the bight of the larger rope in a figure-of-eight pattern.

Old sailing lore

WHIPPING, to prevent the unravelling of the end of a rope. Take several turns of spun-yarn, &c. round the end of the rope, and lay one end under the four first turns, and the other end under the four last turns, and haul tight. Another method is, to knot every turn on the contrary side of the rope, hauling it tight, and finishing the last turn with a reef-knot.

William Falconer's *Dictionary of the Marine*

Zeppelin bend

The name of the Zeppelin bend shows how specific some knot designs can be. This knot was designed specifically to hold down airships. The beauty of the knot is that it is secure and does not jam.

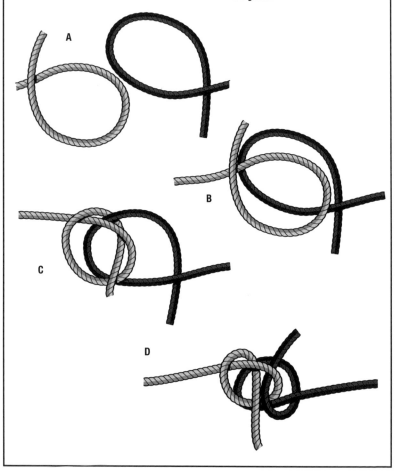

Adjustable bend

The adjustable bend is a type of bend in which two ropes are joined together, with the added advantage that the length of the joined ropes can be adjusted by tightening the knot as necessary.

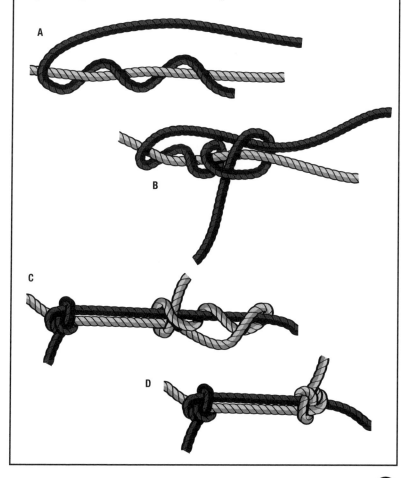

A

B

C

D

Common whipping

The common whipping is the simplest form of whipping and the rope does not need to be unlaid in the process. Although its advantage is its simplicity, it can also easily work loose.

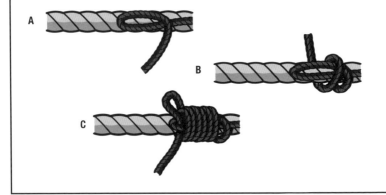

Sailmaker's whipping

This version of whipping is very secure and it is designed for a three-stranded rope. The sailmaker's whipping can be made without any additional tools.

To begin, open a three-stranded rope and loop some whipping twine round one of the strands. Leave the head of the loop hanging free and loose. Then close the strands and begin to wind the thread tightly round the rope. Then take the loop head and pass it over the end of the strand it lies between. Next pull the short tail so that the loop is drawn tight on the strand and against the whipping. Tie the twine at the top with a reef knot, pulling it tight.

Palm and needle whipping

For this form of whipping you will need a 'palm' – a leather and metal hand protection featuring a strap and buckle – and a needle. Thread the needle and push it through one strand of the rope. Then wind the thread round the end of the rope and push the needle through the end of the rope again. Now take the whipping twine over the length of the whipping and insert the needle through the rope. Pull the whipping twine through until it is tight and repeat the process to make a frapping turn. Then pass the needle through the frapping turns and under one frapping turn. Then take the twine over both frapping turns and under another frapping turn. Next push the needle right through the knot, pulling tightly enough so that the knot on the frapping turns is pulled into the braids of the rope. Then cut off any loose ends.

Palm and needle whipping

Palm and needle whipping is particularly appropriate for natural fibre rope, but can be used for other types of rope as well. It is probably the most durable of all kinds of whipping and is made using a needle and a leather safety palm.

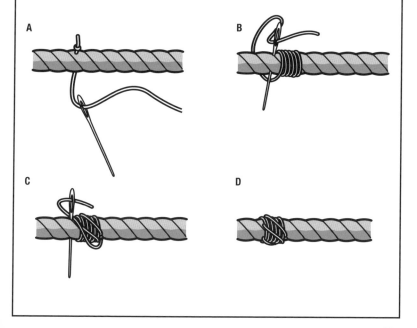

A

B

C

D

Sailmaker's whipping

The sailmaker's whipping is a highly secure and reliable form of whipping and involves both diagonal threading as well as whipping. It is almost as secure and reliable as the palm and needle whipping.

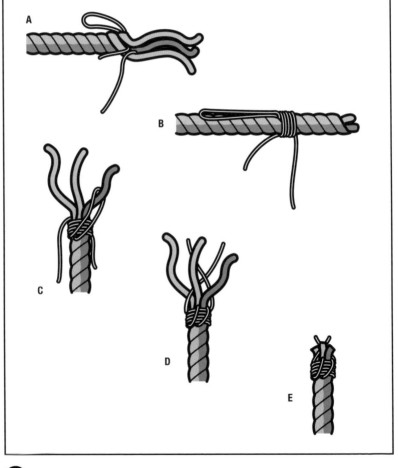

A

B

C

D

E

Old sailing lore

FRAPPING. Taking several turns round the middle of a lashing, or any number of ropes, and drawing the several parts tight together.

LINES. Cordage smaller than ropes, and formed of two or more fine strands of hemp; as HOUSE-LINE, made of three strands, used to seize blocks into their straps and the clues of sails; and to marl the skirts of sails to their bolt-ropes, &c. LOG-LINE, made of three or more strands, and used for the log, &c. MARLINE, made of two strands, and used for the same purposes as house-line.

SPLICING. Joining one rope to another, by interweaving their ends, or uniting the end of a rope into another part of it. There are different sorts of splices, viz. the CUNT-SPLICE, which forms an eye in the middle of a rope: the EYE-SPLICE forms an eye or circle at the end of a rope on itself, or round a block, &c. The LONG-SPLICE is made to rejoin a rope or ropes intended to reeve through a block without encreasing its size: the SHORT-SPLICE is made by untwisting the ends of a rope, or of two ropes, and placing the strands of one between those of the other. The TAPERED-SPLICE is chiefly used on cables, and is made as the short-splice, but is gradually tapered toward each end, by cutting away some of the rope-yarns, and is served over: the DRAWING-SPLICE, is a splice used for joining cables together, and is esteemed the best for this purpose, as it may be readily undone.

The Elements and Practice of Rigging and Seamanship

Old sailing lore

STANDING PART OF A ROPE, (in the making of knots, &c.) means the principal part of a rope, in contra-distinction to the end by which the knot is formed; or it may be said to be that part of a rope which is at rest, and is acted upon by the end.

STOPPERS. Short ropes, used to check the cable, suspend weighty bodies, and retain the shrouds, &c. in a fixed position, after being damaged, or otherwise. ANCHOR-STOPPERS are used to suspend the anchor, when catted: BITT-STOPPERS are those stoppers used to check the cable: DECK-STOPPERS are used to retain the cable when the ship is riding at anchor: DOG-STOPPERS are used as additional securities when the ship is riding in heavy gales, or bringing up a ship with much sternway, to prevent the cable from snapping at the bitts, and to ease the deck-stoppers: WING-STOPPERS are used for the same purposes as dog-stoppers: SHROUD-STOPPERS are used to confine a shroud together, when damaged, or shot. FORE-TACK, and SHEET, STOPPERS, are for securing the tacks and sheets, till belayed.

The Elements and Practice of Rigging and Seamanship

BIGHT, (balant, Fr. bygan, Sax. to bend) the double part of a rope when it is folded, in contradistinction to the end: as, her anchor hooked the bight of our cable, i. e. caught any part of it between the ends. The bight of his cable has swept our anchor; that is, the double part of the cable of another ship, as she ranged about, has entangled itself under the stock or fluke of our anchor.

COILING, (rouer, Fr.) implies a sort of serpentine winding of a cable or other rope, that it may occupy a small space in the ship. Each of the windings of this sort is called a fake, and one range of fakes upon the same line is called a tier; there are generally from five to seven fakes in a tier, and three or four tiers in the whole length of the cables. This, however, depends on the extent of the fakes. The smaller ropes employed about the sails are coiled upon cleats at sea, to prevent their being entangled amongst one another in traversing, contracting, or extending the sails.

GUY, a rope used to keep steady any weighty body whilst it is hoisting or lowering, particularly when the ship is shaken by a tempestuous sea.

Guy is likewise a large slack rope, extending from the head of the main-mast to the head of the fore-mast, and having two or three large blocks fastened to the middle of it. This is chiefly employed to sustain the tackle used to hoist in and out the cargo of a merchant ship, and is accordingly removed from the mast-heads as soon as the vessel is laden or delivered.

HAWSER, a large rope which holds the middle degree between the cable and tow-line, in any ship whereto it belongs, being a size smaller than the former, and as much larger than the latter.

William Falconer's *Dictionary of the Marine*

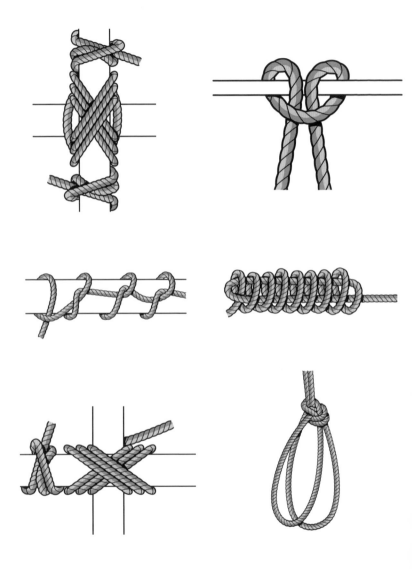

Contents

. . . .

The huge variety of knots and their various uses shows just how important knots are in a range of practical activities. Learning even some of these knots gives you a big advantage.

6

The knots listed in this chapter are arranged by type and represent some of the most commonly used knots across the range.

Directory of Knots

Bends

Bends are commonly used for joining two lines, ropes or pieces of string together.

Adjustable bend

Featured on pages 214, 217

Albright special

Featured on pages 129–131

Ashley's bend

Featured on pages 210, 212

Blood knot

Featured on pages 127, 128

Carrick bend

Featured on pages 188–9, 192

Double fisherman's knot

Featured on pages 65, 69

Double grinner knot

Featured on pages 207, 211

Fisherman's bend/anchor bend

Featured on pages 31, 177

Fisherman's knot/anchor knot

Featured on pages 26, 65, 68

Gaff topsail halyard bend

Featured on pages 175, 176

Heaving line bend

Featured on pages 167, 172, 203, 205

Hunter's bend

Featured on pages 210, 213

Racking bend
Featured on pages 210, 215

Sheet bend
Featured on pages 17, 71, 75

Square knot
Featured on pages 57, 58

Surgeon's knot

Featured on pages 126, 127

Tape knot/water knot
Featured on pages 71, 73

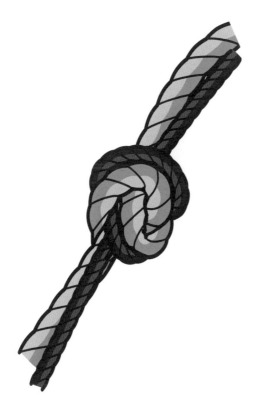

Three-way sheet bend

Featured on pages 114, 115

Zeppelin bend

Featured on pages 210, 214, 216

Binding Knots

Binding knots can be used for lashing poles together or securing sails.

Chain-stitch lashing

Featured on pages 114, 116

Common whipping
Featured on pages 214, 218

Constrictor knot
Featured on pages 192–3, 196–7

Diagonal lashing
Featured on pages 28–9, 100–1, 106

Palm and needle whipping

Featured on pages 218–9

Round lashing
Featured on pages 104, 106

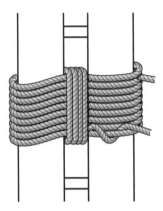

Sailmaker's whipping
Featured on pages 214, 218, 220

Sheer lashing

Featured on pages 30, 106, 108–9

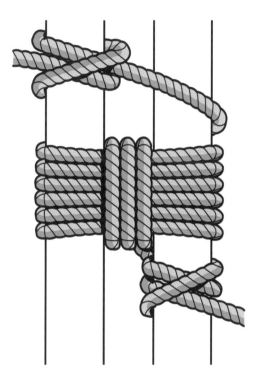

Spade-end knot

Featured on pages 136–7, 138

Square lashing
Featured on pages 27, 98, 102–3

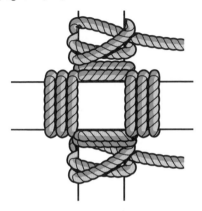

Surgeon's knot
Featured on pages 126, 127

Braid

Braid involves intertwining strands to make a thicker and stronger rope.

Eight-strand square plait braid

Featured on page 120

Coils

It is vital to be able to coil rope to keep it secure and readily available for use.

Chain coil

Featured on page 41

Cleat coil

Featured on pages 167, 169

Common coil

Featured on pages 167, 168

Double hank

Featured on page 41

Gasket coil

Featured on pages 167, 170

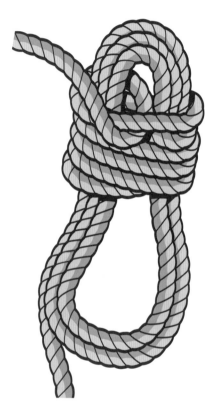

Mountaineer's coil

Featured on page 41

Rucksack coil

Featured on page 41

Stowage coil

Featured on pages 167, 171

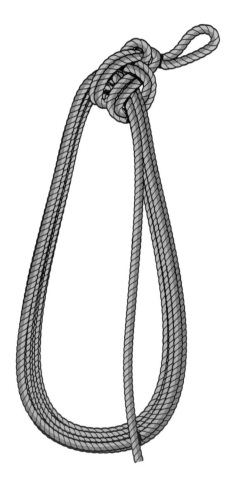

Hitches

Hitches are used to attach a rope to a solid object such as a ring or pole.

Bachmann knot

Featured on pages 56, 57

Barrel sling
Featured on pages 111, 113

Becket hitch
Featured on pages 188, 191

Boom hitch

Featured on pages 175, 177, 180–1

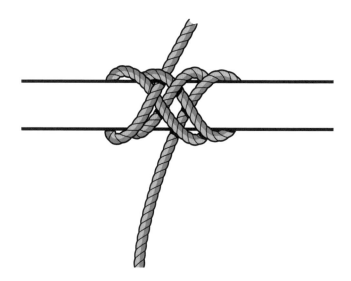

Cat's paw
Featured on pages 177, 182–3

Chain hitch

Featured on page 165

Clinch knot

Featured on pages 137, 139

Clove hitch
Featured on pages 69, 70

Diamond hitch

Featured on pages 115–6, 117

Draw hitch/highwayman's hitch

Featured on page 193

French Prusik knot

Featured on pages 55, 57

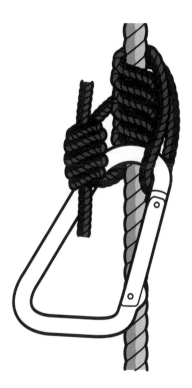

Groundline hitch

Featured on pages 131, 133

Half-blood knot

Featured on pages 132, 133

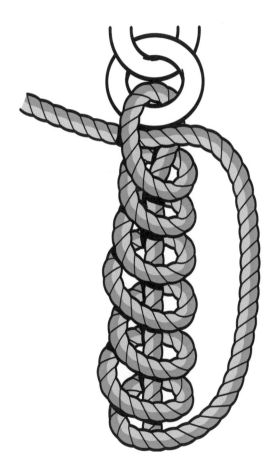

Halter hitch

Featured on pages 177, 185

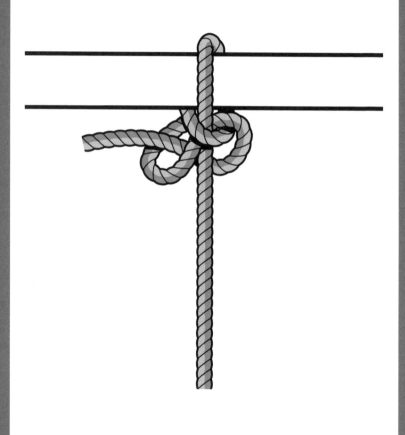

Italian hitch/Munter hitch
Featured on pages 71, 72

Jansik special
Featured on pages 133, 135

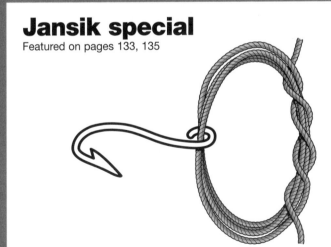

Klemheist

Featured on pages 53, 54

Kreuzklem

Featured on pages 54, 57

Lark's foot/cow hitch/ ring hitch

Featured on pages 76, 77

Lighterman's hitch/ towboat hitch

Featured on pages 189–192, 194–5

Mooring hitch
Featured on pages 177, 186

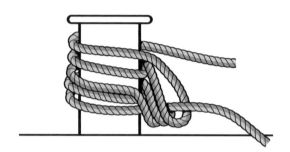

Ossel knot
Featured on pages 175, 178–9

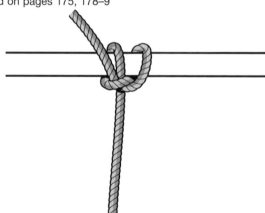

Palomar knot

Featured on pages 133, 134

Rolling hitch

Featured on pages 31, 106–107

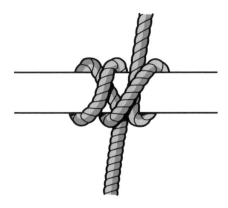

Round turn and two half hitches

Featured on pages 61, 64

Simple hitch/half-hitch

Featured on pages 187, 189

Timber hitch

Featured on pages 32, 105, 106

Trucker's hitch

Featured on pages 193, 199

True lover's knot
Featured on pages 133, 137

Turle knot
Featured on pages 133, 136

Loop Knots

Loops can be created either at the end of a line or along its length.

Alpine knot/butterfly knot

Featured on pages 71, 74

Bimini twist

Featured on pages 142–3, 144–5

Blood-dropper knot

Featured on pages 141, 143

Bowline

Featured on pages 33, 65

Bowline on the bight

Featured on pages 65, 67

Double overhand loop

Featured on pages 137–8, 140

Double overhand sliding loop

Featured on pages 139, 141

Englishman's loop
Featured on pages 139, 141, 142

Figure-of-eight loop

Featured on pages 33, 60, 61

Figure-of-eight on a bight

Featured on pages 46, 60

Fireman's chair knot

Featured on pages 111, 112

Frost knot
Featured on pages 77, 84

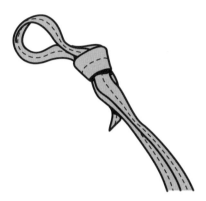

Jury knot
Featured on p.163, 174, 175

Overhand loop
Featured on pages 29, 57, 61

Wireman's knot
Featured on pages 77, 82

Miscellaneous

There are a variety of knots that have very specific uses.

Linfit knot

Featured on page 129

Plank sling

Featured on pages 112, 114

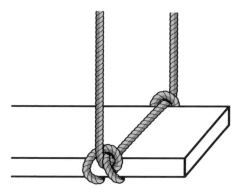

Versatackle

Featured on pages 118–9

Shortening

A shortening knot is useful to strengthen part of a rope that is frayed.

Sheepshank

Featured on pages 172, 173

Splices

Splices are used for joining two bits of rope together for interweaving their strands.

Backsplice

Featured on pages 203, 204

Eye splice
Featured on page 200

Long splice
Featured on pages 195, 202

Short splice

Featured on pages 193, 195, 201

Stopper Knots

Stopper knots are used to stop rope slipping through objects or for providing hand-holds.

Crown knot

Featured on pages 207, 208–9

Figure-of-eight knot

Featured on pages 57, 59

Monkey's fist
Featured on pages 203, 205, 206

Multiple overhand knot
Featured on page 14

Overhand knot
Featured on pages 21, 61, 62

Stevedore's knot
Featured on pages 187–8, 190

Stopper knot
Featured on pages 61, 63

Wall knot
Featured on page 207

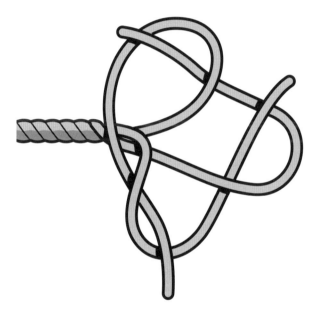

GLOSSARY AND FINAL NOTES

Abseil—to descend from a higher point using a doubled rope that normally runs through a friction device or is coiled round the body

Belay—to fix a rope round an anchor, such as a rock, in order to secure it

Bend—where two pieces of rope are joined together

Bight—a loop of rope

Block—a pulley, or system of pulleys, used on a boat to control lines

Bowsprit—a spar that points out from the bow of a ship to which forestays are fastened

Cleat—a T-shaped object, usually made of metal, to which a rope can be attached

Fast-rope—a rope often used by military personnel to descend from a helicopter to the ground below

Fid—a cone-shaped spike that is used for splicing rope

Frapping—binding action around the middle of a lashing to pull the parts of the lashing together

Halyard—a rope that is used for raising and lowering sails on a boat or ship

Hitch—a knot that is used to attach a rope temporarily to an object, such as a spar or a ring

Jib—a triangular sail that is forward of the mast

Jury rig—a makeshift rigging often set up after a mainmast has broken

Karabiner—a usually metal closure with a lock used by rock climbers and for other applications

Leeward—the side of a boat away from the wind

Line—a length of rope used on board a boat or ship

Loop—a length of rope formed in a loop to tether a boat or form other attachments

Luff—the edge of a sail that is nearest to the mast

Marlinespike—pointed tool made from metal that is used to separate rope strands

Mizzen mast—the mast aft, or behind, the mainmast in a ship

Painter—rope attached to a boat for mooring purposes

Protection—term used to describe anchors placed by rock climbers to restrain fellow climbers should they fall

Rappel—this is an alternative term for abseil (see above)

Sheet—the name given to ropes attached to the lower corners of sails

Shrouds—a set of ropes that supports the mast of a ship

Spinnaker—large three-cornered sail used when running before the wind and attached in front of the main sail

Splice—to join two ropes by interweaving the strands

Standing part—static part of a rope or cord

Stay—a line on a ship that supports a mast either from in front (forestay) or behind (backstay)

Stopper—a type of knot tied to prevent a rope or line passing through a gap, such as a block or ring

Whip—to bind rope spirally with twine or thread

Winch—a circular device with a rotating drum and crank handle used for hauling-in ropes

Working end—part of the rope that is used in the active tying of knots

Yards—horizontal pieces of timber supporting sails on a ship

Rope advice

Official advice from the British Mountaineering Council about ropes

1. Climbing ropes slow the falling climber by stretching – by doing so they reduce the forces on the climber and their protection.

2. Low-stretch ropes are ideal for rigging and abseiling. With less stretch but harder wearing, they must never be used for lead climbing.

3. Walkers ropes are for emergencies only – used as the absolute last resort to overcome short rocky steps in descent, or to help cross a river. Also used to safeguard walking across glaciated terrain.

4. Check your rope before each and every use – run it through your hands whilst visually checking it for damage and deformities.

5. Climbing ropes very rarely break – usually only if loaded over an edge or if exposed to chemicals such as acids.

6. Ropes and belay devices should be compatible. New, thin or slick ropes may be particularly difficult to hold during a fall or when lowering or abseiling. Beware, and always check a new combination before using in anger. Wet and icy ropes may be much harder to control.

7. Storing a rope in a bag and regularly cleaning it using a rope brush and water can extend its life dramatically.

8. Climbing ropes come in single, double or twin format. Single ropes are ideal for beginners, sport climbing and easy mountaineering.

9. Double ropes are the classic choice for traditional climbing and more difficult mountaineering/long routes. Twin ropes which are unpopular in the UK, are ideal for long sport climbs.

10. A climbing rope with a low impact force will stretch more in a fall, putting less force on the top piece of protection.

Karabiners

In Europe, karabiners are manufactured to European Standard EN12275.
They are divided into six different categories according to their intended use:

1. Type B—Basic

This is usually on offset D-shape with either a locking or non-locking gate, which can either be solid or wire. Ways of locking the gate include the screwgate and automatic locking gates. Locking gates are normally used in circumstances in which safety and security is paramount, such as a belay anchor.

2. Type D—Directional

This type of karabiner has a captive or semi-captive sling to ensure the loading is along a particular axis.

3. Type X—Oval

These tend to be weaker than Type D karabiners, but have the advantage of being stable under a load.

4. Type H—HMS

This type of karabiner is specifically designed for belaying and has extra width.

5. Type K—Klettersteig

These karabiners are equipped with an automatically locking gate and tend to be larger than normal. They are specifically designed for use on Via Ferrata lanyards.

6. Type Q—Quicklink

These karabiners are designed for maximum security and come with a screw closure. They are often used as part of an abseil set-up.

Useful websites

American Sail Training Association: www.sailtraining.org
British Mountaineering Council: www.thebmc.co.uk
British Mountaineering Guides: www.bmg.org.uk
Historic Naval Ships Association: www.hnsa.org
International Guild of Knot Tyers: www.igkt.net
Royal Marines: www.royalnavy.mod.uk/royalmarines
Royal Yachting Association: www.rya.org.uk
Sail Training International: www.sailtraininginternational.org
Scouting Resources UK: www.scoutingresources.org.uk
Tall Ships: www.tallships.org
US Army Mountain Warfare School
US Army Northern Warfare Training Center: www.wainwright.army.mil
US Marine Corps Mountain Warfare Training Center: www.mwtc.usmc.mil

INDEX

M